D1295938

The Crocodile by the Door

The Crocodile by the Door

The story of a house, a farm and a family

SELINA GUINNESS

PENGUIN
IRELAND

PENGUIN IRELAND

Published by the Penguin Group
Penguin Ireland, 25 St Stephen's Green, Dublin 2, Ireland
(a division of Penguin Books Ltd)
Penguin Books Ltd, 80 Strand, London WC2R ORL, England
Penguin Group (USA) Inc., 375 Hudson Street, New York, New York 10014, USA
Penguin Group (Australia), 250 Camberwell Road, Camberwell, Victoria 3124, Australia
(a division of Pearson Australia Group Pty Ltd)
Penguin Group (Canada), 90 Eglinton Avenue East, Suite 700, Toronto, Ontario, Canada M4P 2Y3
(a division of Pearson Penguin Canada Inc.)
Penguin Books India Pvt Ltd, 11 Community Centre, Panchsheel Park, New Delhi – 110 017, India
Penguin Group (NZ), 67 Apollo Drive, Rosedale, Auckland 0632, New Zealand
(a division of Pearson New Zealand Ltd)
Penguin Books (South Africa) (Pty) Ltd, Block D, Rosebank Office Park,
181 Jan Smuts Avenue, Parktown North, Gauteng 2193, South Africa

Penguin Books Ltd, Registered Offices: 80 Strand, London WC2R ORL, England

www.penguin.com

First published 2012
003

Copyright © Selina Guinness, 2012

The moral right of the author has been asserted

Set in 12/14.75pt Dante
Typeset by Palimpsest Book Production Limited, Falkirk, Stirlingshire
Printed in Great Britain by Clays Ltd, St Ives plc

A CIP catalogue record for this book is available from the British Library

ISBN: 978-1-844-88157-4

www.greenpenguin.co.uk

MIX
Paper from
responsible sources
FSC
www.fsc.org   FSC™ C018179

Penguin Books is committed to a sustainable
future for our business, our readers and our planet.
This book is made from Forest Stewardship
Council™ certified paper.

ALWAYS LEARNING   **PEARSON**

For Colin

Prologue

Pulling on his wellingtons for the walk down the Lawn, our front field, Liam tells me he is a country boy. 'How's lambing going?' he asks, and I answer him easily, as if we've been farming for years.

We stroll down past the lime tree towards the thicket of gorse at the end of the Lawn. It is a clear, cold, windy day, and the sun picks out the various structures sticking up like pegs in front of Lambay Island: the Dundrum Luas bridge, the Belfield water tower, RTÉ's television mast, and the candy-striped chimneys at the Pigeon House, a grey plume of smoke scudding out towards the bay.

'I can see why you'd want to preserve that view,' Liam says, stopping to admire it as his colleagues have done before him. 'They knew how to site a house in those days.'

It's true. The whites and darks of the city stipple the middle distance. In the foreground, beyond the gorse, are the St Thomas fields, which Liam's boss, the property developer Bernard McNamara, bought two years ago from our neighbour Major McDowell. My uncle Charles had sold those fields to pay rates in 1976; until then, the St Thomas lands had served as a sister farm to Tibradden. Chris Keogh's cattle graze below us in the long field beside the River Glin. The banks are densely wooded with silver firs, larches, sweet chestnuts and oaks, all planted by my great-great-grandfather, Thomas Hosea Guinness.

I

'Are those the trees you're concerned about?' Liam asks me, pointing to the waving ribbon of treetops where rooks are rising and resettling in the wind. 'Yes. You can see that, though our land stops here, the planting is continuous right the way along the length of the stream. It traces the line of the original avenue from our house down to the old mill at Kilmashogue Bridge.'

In fact, the woods step on beyond St Thomas's fields. They link this estate into a two-hundred-year-old chain of parklands at Marlay, St Enda's and Rathfarnham Castle, planted along the Dodder tributaries to culminate at Bushy Park.

A week ago, through a neighbour, I got my hands on a map that McNamara's company has been circulating among the committee of a nearby golf club. They want to buy the club's current course to build houses, and hope to persuade members to move to a new location up the hill at St Thomas and Tibradden – a site that would include twenty acres of land they're trying to buy from me. The A4 laminate shows a preliminary plan for the course they intend to develop on these lands, should they succeed in acquiring them. This palate-teaser for the club's committee has made me queasy with anxiety.

The designer has digitally superimposed the position of all eighteen holes on an aerial photograph; the result is an eerie collage of the real and the purely speculative. The photograph must have been taken at the height of summer: the beeches are in full spread, the silage already harvested in the adjacent field. At the bottom right-hand corner, a lorry is carrying a load up Tibradden Road from the roundabout at Kilmashogue Mill; traffic looks sparse on the M50. The shot could have been taken from one of the helicopters that pass hourly over our house, or simply transposed from Google Earth into whatever software package the designer used.

The digital overlay of the golf course renders familiar land almost unrecognizable. The hedges, fences and walls that separate fields have been effaced, so the only recognizable features left within the zone of the golf course are the canopies of trees. The stream that Liam and I are walking beside appears on the map artificially blue, and widens into two new lakes. Great swathes of the woodland running alongside it will have to be felled to clear a path for the six holes that are to be played across water. Pea-green blotches represent fairways; green globes, like Brussels sprouts, signify new planting schemes. Black lines show the direction of play, criss-crossed by faint contour lines superimposed, the legend says, from 'a topographic plan supplied by the client'.

It came as a shock to see the twenty acres McNamara's company wishes to buy from me incorporated seamlessly into this proposal, to see fairways traversing the acres our sheep still graze. If this map is in local circulation, my neighbours might assume it is a done deal. Not that this would cause any surprise: many of them have been expecting me to sell the farm ever since my uncle died three years ago.

But there is no deal yet. Negotiations have stalled over my insistence on a covenant that would compel McNamara's company, and any subsequent owners, to maintain the mixed woodland along the River Glin in perpetuity. The wording has been kicked back and forth between my solicitor and theirs for several months. Liam is here today hoping to persuade me to give up the covenant in entirety.

'The bank don't like it,' he says bluntly. 'They won't accept you placing any restriction on their title. It's not even up to us any more.'

I have no ready reply. I realize that the covenant expresses something much deeper than my desire to preserve the trees:

it is an attempt to bind the purchaser to a story that is mine to tell, not theirs.

It is also an expression of ambivalence about the whole idea of selling any of these fields. For although I am their legal owner, I am not yet sure that I am morally entitled to sell land I still think of as my uncle's. Charles never put me under any obligation towards him or Tibradden. He saw that I could assume custodianship for the place he loved only if I loved it independently of him and came to it with my own sense of its future. Now I understand that I am taking part in a long history I must not break lightly.

The trees below us were planted to please a woman, Mary Davis, when she married Thomas Hosea Guinness in 1859 and transferred her land into his name. Her ancestors were originally wool-combers, guild-members in the Liberties, making their living from trading the wool they produced here as tenants in the eighteenth century. It is only through becoming a farmer myself that I've learned to appreciate how sweat creates an attachment beyond talk of property and prices. Something in me baulks at the idea of golfers parading at leisure over a legacy of dirt and toil.

Wait, I want to say to Liam, wait until I've caught up with all that's happened these past few years; then I might be prepared to sell. But everyone tells me that property developers don't wait. I must snap at the enormous sum they're offering while Dublin's property market is still red-hot. 'Top dollar,' the estate agent keeps repeating. 'You'll never be offered this price again.' I need the money badly to restore the house and farm. The St Thomas fields below us are already in McNamara's hands; a covenant over trees is a very slight protection against change.

Liam is looking at me now, trying to gauge whether his account of the bank's intransigence has made an impression.

He's not as cocky as his colleagues. I'm so tired of bargaining it would be a relief to let him get his way. But, in the end, I can't.

'I guess you'll just have to keep talking to them, then,' I say, and turn to lead the way back up towards the house.

I.

I'm coming back to Tibradden, to live with Charles again. I've driven down from Belfast with boxes stacked on the back seat; Colin will follow with the rest of our belongings when his term has finished.

The sunlight picks out the carious gaps between the capping stones on the Calfpark wall as I drive up Mutton Lane. I indicate left, and sidle in through the white farm gate onto the rubble drive. The window of the gate-lodge is open. Through it I can hear Susie Kirwan shouting at Joseph, her son, over the noise of the television. Joe, Susie's husband, has planted wallflowers in a bed beside the house. Nettles and frothy white elder bushes throng the lower reaches of the drive, except for a small clearing behind the cedars where the tractor stands, its bucket raised. Around the bend, the rhododendrons have shed a carpet of crushed red petals I don't feel prodigal enough to merit. Beside me, the patch of mossy lawn we still call the tennis court has just been mown.

For the past seven years, since Muriel Jackson, the housekeeper, retired, my uncle Charles has been living alone at Tibradden. I find him sitting in a deck-chair in the porch, waiting for me. He could have been sitting here since lunchtime. He puts down his paper as I draw up and beams at me. 'Hello, darling,' he says. 'How lovely to see you.' I kiss him and let him lead the way inside.

I set my coat and bag down on a chair and look around the

hall. Nothing seems to have been touched since I was here last. The big copper jug in which my grandmother once arranged honesty and everlasting flowers sits on the marble-topped chest inside the front door. Boxes of light-bulbs poke out of the top. Beside the jug grins the crocodile, car keys dangling from a front incisor. My great-grandfather's brother, Henry, shot it in Persia and sent the head to a taxidermist in Piccadilly to be turned into a letterbox for his six siblings at home.

When I was a child, Charles used to lift me up to slide papers through the brass slot in its gullet. That such an exotic beast could become merely another item of household furniture did not surprise me: Tibradden was a place where astonishing things were everyday items. You might come across anything from a blue kimono embroidered with gold dragons to a box containing my grandfather's prosthetic right arm. These items could be worn, handled, used as props in whatever make-believe world we cared to create; we were as free to play with them as we were with our own Lego.

'All post,' I remember my uncle explaining, 'used to leave Tibradden through the crocodile. You see, here at the back,' and he would swivel the head sideways, 'is the door for the postman. Only he had the key. When there were lots of brothers and sisters living in this house, they didn't want anyone to know whom they were writing to, so they posted their letters in here. Look, like this.'

He would take a discarded envelope and lift me up to push it through the slot. I'd watch as he turned the crocodile's head fully round to unlock and open the door. Once more he'd pick me up so that I could reach in and triumphantly pull the envelope out for his applause.

The crocodile still sits here by the door, like a guardian of the house, or a god to be propitiated, its jaws open for whatever intimacy I might care to throw its way. It serves as a kind of cloakroom where you can check in your secrets, permitting you to proceed light and unencumbered to take tea in the drawing room. In this house, there is a way of talking that repels disclosure while remaining kind and affectionate; we observe a generous distance from each other at the risk of lapsing into silence. The important thing is not to intrude too much on the patterns of the day. My uncle used to start humming tunelessly if a visitor introduced a topic he judged difficult for himself or my grandmother. Money was one trigger, the human body another. My mother used to set off entire song-cycles when I became a teenager.

Now that I am moving in with Charles, I know I must practise the discretion symbolized by the crocodile and respect my uncle's privacy. But this might not be easy. My uncle has spent the past seven years inhabiting his house free of female interference. Neither he nor the house looks well on it. Dust and inertia have settled over all. For years, Charles, who has just turned seventy, has stepped round difficulties that can no longer be deferred. When he suggested, two years ago, that Colin and I share the house with him, he must have known that things would have to change, but I doubt he has anticipated the scale of works required to update the house to meet our needs. Most of these are physical: the leaking roof must be fixed, the lead-wiring and rotting window boards replaced, the flammable chimneys cleaned – the list goes on. All of these will take time and money, but they will also require negotiation of much larger questions about the future of Tibradden. I am not sure how to broach these over the coming months without triggering the humming. And yet, on several occasions, my uncle has reminded me, 'You pretty well started out your life here.' This is as close as he can come to saying I should consider his house my home.

*

A fortnight after I was born, my parents came to stay at Tibradden for a few weeks so that Charles and my grandmother, Kitty, could help look after me. It was a difficult time for everyone: the household was still in mourning for my grandfather, Owen, who had unexpectedly passed away in his sleep just two weeks before I was born. I had colic, but my grandmother mistook my cries for hunger and insisted on adding solids to my feed when I was just a month old. My father took his wife's side, and fought with his mother. Charles boiled kettles and made bottles, and kept out of the disputes. Later he'd remember this as a happy time.

For the next eleven years I had a fairly conventional suburban childhood. Our bungalow, located in an estate a few miles downhill from Tibradden and a few miles uphill from the Irish Sea, was still very new in 1972 when my parents moved there from Churchtown, in need of an extra bedroom now my mother was pregnant again. My younger brother, Niall, and I went to the local primary school, rode bikes and played out on the greens with all the other kids on the road.

On Sundays we donned our best bib and tucker and went for lunch to Tibradden. Charles was my father's only sibling, his senior by nine years. He and Kitty sat at either end of the dining-room table. I sat on one side, next to Niall, while Dad and Mum sat on the other. When you rang the bell Muriel, dressed in her starched white pinafore with crossed straps at the back over her black blouse, pushed the trolley in. You sat still and were served by Muriel or my grandmother out of stoneware dishes onto willow-pattern plates. The vegetables all came from the kitchen garden where Paddy Flanagan, the gardener, grew them from seed. One of the adults would cut up our meat because the bone-handled knives were blunt, or so they said. As I grew taller I used to slip off a shoe and shine up the ball-and-claw foot of the dining-room table. Afterwards, if we'd been good, we'd be given squares of Dairy Milk from the chocolate drawer in the drawing room.

When I was nine, my parents separated. In Ireland, in the early 1980s, this made us the object of whispered concern in our suburb. My parents managed their separation without obvious rancour. Dad moved into a flat in Ranelagh, which he thought shabby and we thought sophisticated on account of the intercom system and lift. There was a waste-grinder in the kitchen sink into which you could feed whole eggshells. We went to stay with him every other weekend. On wet Sundays his chess friends would come over and empty their match-boxes to teach us how to play poker and pontoon. Other times he'd take us on outings to historic sites or, better still, the races and Bray amusements, before returning to cook dinner from Robert Carrier's *Great Dishes of the World*. We were his guinea-pigs, he told us, for future dinner-parties. Niall and I poked snails from tins into empty shells and pasted them with garlic butter, before tucking into Steak Diane.

My mother got a part-time job in a city-centre art gallery, where Niall and I played in the stockroom after school. Sometimes she would walk us up to the Natural History Museum and leave me in charge of my brother for an hour while she returned to work in Lincoln Place. It was the grandeur and absurdity of the 'Dead Zoo' that made it so enticing: the Arctic hare yellowing in its tundra landscape below the cast-iron colonnades, the glass cabinet of hummingbirds reached by a set of spiral stairs. Here and there were signs that these animals were as familiar to others as Tibradden's crocodile was to us: the crease inside the giraffe's foreleg where the stitches holding the hide together had been surreptitiously picked apart; the spot on the zebra's bottom rubbed bare.

For secondary school, my parents intended to send us both to St Columba's College, on the slopes of Kilmashogue; from the front steps of Tibradden, you could hear the chapel bell. The school grounds were familiar territory. Uncle Charles taught French and German there, and when we were very little he used to take us to see the pig that was housed in a sty at the bottom of the stable block. On hot summer days, we swam in the outdoor pool with its view of the cricket pitch, Marlay Park, and the city beyond. I was expected to board, but I stubbornly refused to consider it. This presented my mother with a problem.

By the time I was eleven she had left the gallery and become an independent art dealer. She now travelled to auctions across Britain and Ireland looking for paintings she might sell on. In a year's time, Niall would become a boarder. She and her partner, David, would need to travel for a week or ten days at a time, up and down the motorways of England, searching for undiscovered Irish art in regional auction houses. It was what she had to do to earn a living. She could not commit to being home to collect me from school.

I don't know whether the solution was one Mum hatched in consultation with my father, or whether Kitty and Charles stepped forward to propose I stay with them. In any case, it was decided I would live at Tibradden. My uncle could take me to school each morning in time for chapel, and he could return to collect me in the evening. 'You've always loved staying at Tibradden,' my mother assured me, in a way that made me question, for the first time, whether this was absolutely true. 'Besides, Kitty treats you as the daughter she never had.' This felt like too big a confidence for me to bear. I felt as if I was being handed over as some kind of trophy to the victors of a battle I hadn't realized was being waged above my head. My mother had brought me to Tibradden at birth, and now I was being handed back to the house.

*

I remember following Muriel up the stairs. She carried my red suitcase. Instead of going across the landing to the dressing room where I usually stayed when visiting Tibradden, she turned right and disappeared into the small entry outside my uncle's room. I walked on through the door into the bedroom assigned to my father when he was a child. My brother usually slept there on visits, but I had always coveted the wallpaper, with its posies of bluebells arranged between long curling lines of blue ribbon, tied at intervals in bows. It was not a boy's room. Muriel smiled shyly at me as she put the case down and, turning to go out, said, 'There's a hot-water bottle in your bed.'

I opened up the wardrobe. The shelves were stacked with books, but there was some hanging space for my school shirts among the old paisley dressing-gowns. My trousers and jumpers were to be put in the chest of drawers behind the door. Two china Staffordshire dogs, with chipped noses, one missing a foot, served as bookends for another row of novels shelved on top. There were two beds in the room, the old one with its bedposts like twists of barley sugar, and the new one in which I was to sleep. Despite a portable heater, the room was cold.

I took off my socks and shoes. The sisal matting pricked my feet as I walked over to the window. It was September, so behind the forest-green curtains the shutters were latched closed. I stood up on the radiator to open them. The lights of Dublin twinkling beyond the front field emphasized the darkness of the woods along the stream. Our grandmother did not like us to play down there by ourselves, fearing that we might tumble into the waterfalls, but our mother was unconcerned: 'Oh, Kitty, they'll be fine,' she'd say. Released then, Niall and I would run down the rhododendron walk, and duck under the low branches through the wicket gate to clamber onto the swaying bridge and throw sticks into the stream below. We had found beer bottles and the remains of camp fires, and the thought of who might be down in the woods at night made me feel afraid.

Boarding schools rely on the hope that routine can substitute for a mother if the child has a memory of love with which she can lie down and sleep. The days at Tibradden unfolded on this same assumption. At seven each morning Gran made tea in her bedroom and, still dressed in her flannel pyjamas, delivered a cup to Charles and one to me. I drank it suspiciously, blowing aside the thick lumps of cream and the loose tea-leaves that floated on top. Downstairs, just after eight, Charles would bring us each a boiled egg from the pantry. He had bought a Dimplex hotplate specifically for this purpose before I arrived, having till then survived on toast and cereal for breakfast. Our aim was to get into the car and away before the first bell rang for chapel at 8.17 a.m. I had to be seated with the other girls five minutes later, ready to rise to our feet when the boys filed in.

The warden's previous post had been at St Paul's Colonial School for Boys in Darjeeling. It would be fair to describe a good part of the education offered at St Columba's as idiosyncratic. We spent our first term learning Esperanto as a foundation for beginning French in the second. Another teacher tried to teach us Russian through the medium of Irish, of which only a handful of pupils – those of us who'd attended national school – had any knowledge at all. In history, we spent a full year on the French Revolution, nothing else. We translated love poems by Catullus in the cottage known as the Doll's House at the end of the Second Garden while eating fancy biscuits from an assortment box circulated by our Latin master. In biology we copied down perfect diagrams of the human body that we failed to relate to our own. In summer, the chapel doors opened and Widor's Toccata spilled out over the perfect lawns and past the weeping willow where the swallows dipped low. It was all a far remove from Kill-of-the-Grange National School and from life in our bungalow.

I felt angular and awkward, caught between two ways of life. The bands I listened to in my later school years – the Smiths, the Violent Femmes – rejected all that this world stood for: the country houses and ponies from which I was one generation removed but to which I'd been returned as if a native. In the library at the back of the boarding house, I found *Go Ask Alice* among the P. G. Wodehouse and, bizarrely, a biography of Lenin's wife, Krupskaya. I skived off games as best I could and hid out there, reading through the afternoons.

When the school day was finished I took off my black scholar's gown, exchanged it for my coat from the cardboard box on top of my locker and escaped along the gravel paths of the Second Garden. At the bottom of the Whispering Steps, Charles would be waiting in his car, the internal light on as he listened to Radio Four. 'Hello, darling,' he greeted me, as I slipped into the back seat. We usually drove home to Tibradden in silence. Neither of us had much that could be told to the other, then.

The big cow bell that hung on a thick leather strap in the hall rang each evening at half past seven. This was the last note in the first movement of dinner, which was performed each evening to a fixed choreography. The study where I worked was next door to the dumb-waiter. The theme music of *The Archers* wafted up the shaft from the kitchen as dishes clattered in. I'd hear Muriel's feet dragging up the wooden kitchen stairs, then the door banging behind her and, a moment later, the glass in the pantry door rattling as she went in to fetch the trolley. The wheels squeaked their way forward, pausing as she tipped the trolley up to clear the saddle, then turned across the parquet into the flower room. Then came the hollow sound of dinner surfacing: Muriel's red hands methodically hauling in the sisal rope on the right-hand side, while Kathleen, the cook, invisible below, fed up the left-hand one, the pulley squealing all the time. The solid brown dishes were slid onto the top of the trolley, and then the trolley was off, rattling through the hall. The soft sound of the dining-room door being opened, with a pause for the bell, was my cue to appear.

My grandmother settled herself at the far end of the mahogany table, near the trolley, my uncle at the near end. I sat in the middle. We had soup to start, from an Erin packet most nights, except for consommé, which came from a Campbell's tin. Gran taught me to tip the liquid from the silver spoon sideways to my lips and to tilt the soup plate away from me as it emptied. 'Don't slurp,' she'd instruct, not unkindly. We each took a slice of Brennan's white pan from the packet on the trolley, and pasted on butter from a little glass dish, tearing holes in the bread. When we had finished, Gran rang the bell for Muriel, who would come and clear the soup plates away, leaving her mistress to serve the main course from the brown dishes on the hotplate. 'Twice-laid' – a dish assembled from Sunday's roast, the meat mixed with breadcrumbs, onions and left-over gravy and baked again – might follow. Then there would be yoghurt, the Sno plastic tub set in a bowl, eaten with a dessert spoon, or occasionally junket, a milk pudding made with the rennet my grandmother would ask her English visitors to bring her; as with ginger beer, you could not buy it in Ireland.

With every mouthful we sought for some bit of news to stir the still waters. Sometimes Charles would hum to himself, or look at the ceiling and emit a low groan. My grandmother's translucent fingers, the same colour as the pearls she wore daily, thoughtfully tore her bread into pieces en route to her mouth. Occasionally she would grimace as she stirred her soup, and shake her head, and mouth, 'Bah.' I took this to be an expression of pain, although she rarely complained of any ailment more specific than the succession of chills and colds that prevented her from kissing anyone goodbye. These noises were not prompts for conversation, but were indications of internal dialogues with their own turbulent patterns, which were no business of a child.

About three nights a week Charles went out after dinner to committee meetings of the Select Vestry or the School Board of Management or the Forces Help Society or Simpson's Hospital. 'He does such a lot for the parish,' my grandmother would say approvingly, as the front door closed.

I slouched at her feet on the hearth rug in the drawing room, always aware that our best conversations would happen now when she could stare off into the past, forgetting for a moment that I was there with her.

'What do you see in the fire?' she would ask.

'Houses,' I'd reply. 'Burning houses with rafters falling in.'

'I see faces.' She pointed to the flames licking along the underside of a blackened log. 'Look, there's a nose, and if you look along the briquette, you can see two eyes.'

I searched the fire but the faces had gone by the time I looked, as the houses fell in storey upon storey. Into this darkness we had thrown our lists to Father Christmas each year.

Moving me aside, she picked up the small poker and stirred the embers to let the ash fall down through the grate before lifting one of the logs placed against the fender to dry out. She dropped it in at the back, gasping a bit with the effort, but would rather that than allow a child to do it.

'Move back a bit or you'll scorch yourself,' she'd say, resuming her chair. I stroked my shoulder with my left hand and felt the heat from the blaze in my jumper.

The room ticked around us although the grandfather clock had long ago stopped. I picked at the rug and gazed at the fire. She always spoke in her own time.

'Charles is very good,' she said. 'And I mustn't grumble. He is very good to allow me to continue living here with him. It is his house, you know.' She kept looking at her hands, avoiding any query I might have. 'If I leave the room, you must keep the fire guard up, you know that. If anything were to happen, well . . .' She turned her palms out to convey the immeasurable scale of the loss. 'It just costs too much to insure.'

Beyond the lesson that I should take care, there was another melody in what she said. I understood that she had seen a falling off, and yet her eldest son could not be blamed. Books were what interested him, not houses, their maintenance and decoration. To expect otherwise was foolish. The standard to which Tibradden failed to measure up was not, I gathered, that of its earlier days, although my mother used to say that the one time the farm had turned a profit was under my grandmother's stewardship during the war. But what farm didn't make money, then? No, the standard had been set by the house Gran still considered her proper home, Barford Hill, in Warwickshire, a photograph of which hung above her bureau.

Plain and ugly on the outside, inside it had had everything: a splendid oak-panelled dining room, a ballroom, a billiard room, sunny nurseries and somewhere between twenty and thirty bedrooms. Large as Tibradden was, it seemed to me unimaginable that a house might have too many bedrooms to count. Barford Hill was very modern – with its own power plant to feed the central heating and the electric lighting her father had installed – and enjoyed every comfort; my grandmother approved of these things. A spreading cedar stood in the middle of the lawn, its lower boughs arranged like rungs for children to climb. Across the road were stables and a walled kitchen garden, with greenhouses full of grapes, peaches and orchids. During the war, the servants' quarters had been turned into a convalescent hospital for a hundred men.

'Oh, it was lovely,' Gran exclaimed, her voice vivid with its riches and the company of her siblings running to and fro down the corridors.

'What happened to it?' I asked jealously.

'My nephew, Charlie, pulled it down.' She said it without a trace of bitterness. 'After the war, it was simply too difficult to run without the staff, so nobody wanted it. And it was far too expensive to live in.' The cedar tree, though, was still there. One day, if I visited my cousins in Sherborne, they might take me to see it.

I was not sure I would ever visit these cousins, who were several times removed by blood, and even more by nationality, class and politics. News of their activities arrived in weekly letters and made up a large part of the conversation over dinner. Enclosed were clippings from *Tatler* or *Country Life* featuring them at charity balls or togged out in pinks to command the local hunt. They owned horses and dogs and guns, and knew how to shoot and gut pheasants. The girls worked during the winter at ski chalets and completed Cordon Bleu cookery courses in preparation for marriage. Their fathers were members of the Conservative Party who were unsure whether Mrs Thatcher was a good thing. Gran's family visited rarely, and although no reasons were given, I understood this might be because of 'the security situation'. In any case, Tibradden could not offer the same excitements. Mostly guests played bridge, or Gran might invite me to join them for a game of Scrabble after a trip to 'Dublin', as she always called town.

★

To listen to my grandmother's memories of Barford Hill became a complicated pleasure. The implied criticism of Tibradden made me feel defensive of the place that had been her home for more than forty years but that was just becoming my Arcadia. I resented, too, the warmth of her recollections, which seemed to diminish my value as company. The wild-flowers she taught me to identify in W. Keble Martin's field guide had not first been recognized by her in these fields, but in others I would never visit. Yet slowly these thoughts began to dissolve and turn. My grandmother had arrived here once and adopted this house on the hill as her home, as I now would too.

It was Gran who had pointed out the lone palm tree rising above the laurels as evidence that the woods along the stream had once been a formal garden, with ponds. 'Your father and Charles used to fish here in the boat that's now up in the stables,' she told me one day, as we stopped by the marsh to watch a heron pick its way through the leafy shallows. She had sat down on a fallen tree to regain her breath while I poked around in the stream for the tiny mica beads stuck together by caddis fly larvae, which I collected and stored in jars on the front steps waiting for the imago to hatch and fly.

'Do you think we could make ponds here again?' I asked, as I clambered up, jar in hand, the bright water running down my arm.

'It's out of the question.' To my bewilderment, she was cross. She took her own measure before looking up at me. Noting my expression, she continued, 'When they opened the gravel pits up the mountain, your great-grandfather broke his back trying to keep the silt-traps clear. There aren't the men to do it now, in any case.'

It didn't matter to me, really. The pale grey sky fell in through the clearing and rested in pools between the rushes. Every rustling noise in the undergrowth could be a deer or a red squirrel, or, more surprisingly, a fox or badger. Once, my brother had seen men with guns climbing over the fence into the far field. He had hidden behind a tree and watched them pass, and then he'd run back and told us all, and after the adults had exchanged glances, I'd been told not to be afraid, they were probably only hunters out deer-stalking.

On Wednesdays, classes finished at lunchtime. In the brighter months I would get my uncle's permission to come home early, on foot. While the rest were at games, I'd head for the back gate onto Kilmashogue Lane, climb over the wire fence opposite into Featherstone's fields, and make my way to the woods of St Thomas.

Although it now belonged to Major McDowell, the chairman of the *Irish Times* trust, St Thomas used to be the dower house to Tibradden. This history, obscurely felt, allowed me to decide it could not be trespassing to scramble along St Thomas's boundaries. The old avenue began where the walled banks confined the stream to a mill-race, then continued along its course, marked by a line of granite boulders, for at least a mile up the hill to the Lawn in front of Tibradden. I remembered my father walking me along its length when I was very small, and I recalled it as a more impressive road then than it was now. A scraggy colonnade of pollarded beech trees was familiar, and I thought I remembered, too, the three cut-stone arched bridges over which the path led, skirting thickets of brambles along the way. In places, the track would once have been wide enough to accommodate a car. Broken glass and plastic bottles suggested others used it as a shortcut up towards Larch Hill, but I never met anyone else along the way.

'Well, ducks, where have you been?' my uncle would ask, as I slipped in through the drawing-room door in time for tea.

'Oh, just out, exploring,' I'd say, and my grandmother would move back her chair and invite me in to share the warmth of the fire. Curled up on the hearth, my legs tucked under the gate-leg table, I always felt as if I'd come safely home at last.

2.

May 2002

It is hard to retrace those steps, nearly twenty years after I first made my way back to Tibradden from St Columba's, for the line of the old avenue has almost disappeared. The stream has diverted around fallen trees, overflowing the mill race to carve new channels in the soft banks. Evergreen laurels sprawl into the clearings left by larger trees, so that to negotiate the old road requires stepping over trunk and under bough, following as best I can the skeins of wool caught on twig and briar as guides to the new tracks our sheep have made straying between our fields and St Thomas's, concerned only with the quest for sweeter grass. The last stone bridge leads out through a black wrought-iron gate into the long sloping field below the Lawn.

I emerge from the dark shade of the overhanging firs and larches into a sunlit amphitheatre where the view towards Tibradden seems to wait for applause. The house, with its three bays, stands square between the clumped rhododendrons, the epitome of respectability save for the two arched windows above the front door, which shoot up like eyebrows in surprise that any onlooker should have made it this far. It is not, as my mother used to say, a beautiful house, although it does command an impressive view.

Two plain chimney stacks in front hide the two lined up at the rear. Smoke rises from the left-hand one above the drawing room just as a child would draw it. A child, however, would leave the façade paper-white or paint it any shade other than its current rust-streaked, damp-stained grey; the front door and window frames are the same bottle-green as my old school jumper. To the right, a line of cedars steps away along the gravel drive, with an underskirt of rhododendrons that blooms extravagantly crimson against the dark green foliage in spring. To the left, above the line of trees that flanks the stream, rises the shoulder of Kilmashogue, with the head of Tibradden Mountain dozing out of sight behind the court-yard.

The tall and graceful lime tree, planted in the middle of the Lawn before this house was ever built, provides an alternative pivot for the view. Its low boughs supply scratching posts for the few cattle sheltering under it. The strong sweet scent of its flowers attracts swarms of bees, and most afternoons the deer tiptoe out from the woods and rise on their hind legs to steal its aromatic leaves. A copper beech, planted in close as a nursery tree and never cut down, sits in the shadow of the lime. Viewed from the house, the two trees are indistinguishable in the per-fect bell shape described by their branches; in the distance beyond them, the two towers of the Pigeon House poke up from the edge of Dublin Bay.

Since moving back to Tibradden I have begun to be woken at night by dreams that, no matter how they begin, become a film of the lime splitting down the centre and the view slowly tumbling apart in a whirl of disconnected rooms and fields. On stolen afternoons, I have tried to fix each part back into posi-tion by haunting the old drive or the rooms of Henigan's derelict cottage across in the field I know as Marymount. Susie refers to this field as the Nineteen Acres, a reference to the old Irish measure; it is almost twice that size in statute acres. In patches not yet colonized by gorse, I discover stitchwort, bird's foot trefoil, common vetch and wild strawberries. I know they will not last in water, but pick the flowers anyway, recalling how my grandmother's face would soften at the sight of them before she went to find a vase.

A complicated set of considerations has led Colin and me to decide to move in with my uncle. Three years ago we returned to Ireland from England, where Colin had been working and I'd been studying, to take new lecturing jobs. For a couple of years we rented a small flat in Booterstown, on the south side of Dublin, not far from my job at the Dun Laoghaire Institute of Art, Design and Technology. Colin used to take the train to Belfast on Monday morning for his job at Queen's University, and stayed with his parents in Dundonald during the week. This seemed the most sensible arrangement – my job entailed longer terms and more teaching hours than his – but it was hard on him. He spent most evenings in his parents' guest bedroom talking on the phone. I was in Dublin; his three children, Jo, Seamus and Mel, remained in Hull with their mother. He shuttled alternate weekends among us and tried to ignore the strain. When the children came to Dublin for their holidays, our Booterstown flat was not big enough for us all, and so at Charles's suggestion we decamped to Tibradden. In summer, we found old clubs and racquets and footballs and played on the abandoned tennis court. At Christmas, we huddled around the drawing-room fire with Charles and bickered over board games. It was all a shabby replica of idyllic childhoods past.

The question of Tibradden's future had been the subject of a number of family meetings since the mid-1990s. These were organized by my uncle's solicitor and accountant, who were concerned that their client had not updated his will for many years. I had attended several of these meetings, at which Charles made it clear that he wanted only to do what was 'considered right' by the family. Without children of his own, and no other near relatives, the family amounted to my father, my brother and me. At that time, Niall was working in Spain while I was studying in Oxford towards an academic career that might land me anywhere. My father said he was 'too old to take on Tibradden'; besides, he and my stepmother, Rosemary, were very happy living where they were. Tibradden was viewed less as an opportunity than as a burden. When the issue of the estate's value came up, everyone swallowed hard. My uncle struggled to work out how he could be fair to each of us in passing on an asset that none of us could bear to see sold, and yet none of us knew how to manage. Somehow we could not imagine our family without Tibradden at its core. The meetings had stalled at this impasse without, as far as I knew, any new will having been prepared.

My appointment to a permanent lectureship at Dun Laoghaire, and coming home with Colin, had changed things. We asked Charles whether he could spare a site on the grounds for us to build a small wooden house. He chuckled at the idea of us living in a log cabin – and we eventually dropped the idea – but he seemed genuinely pleased that we were planning to come back to Tibradden. About two years ago he suggested that we come and live with him in the main house.

Although grateful for his generous offer, it took us a while to accept. My teaching load and Colin's commuting meant that we had no spare time to begin the project of moving to Tibradden and reclaiming a practical living space from the decades of disrepair and ancestral clutter in the rooms we would need. Come the following summer, I promised, we would move in.

But then at Easter, I received a scholarship to complete the doctoral thesis I'd started at Oxford. It involved a year's career break. It seemed only fair, then, to spare Colin the commute from Dublin to Belfast, so we decided to try out his city for a year. When I told Charles my good news, he went quiet and turned his head away towards the window. 'Of course you must go,' he said firmly, but there were tears in his eyes. I realized only then how lonely he had been, and how our visits with the children, which I had feared were an imposition, had been for him a break in the monotonous task of making up his own days.

'It will only be a year,' I promised him. 'If you still want us next summer, we will come and stay for good.'

In the drawing room, Charles has spread a cloth over the gate-leg table in front of the hearth. On the trolley next to it are a scattering of cutlery, crockery and a biscuit tin. The old Hoover lies next to the sofa like a dejected dog.

He finds me setting out the cups and saucers when he returns with the teapot, trembling a little in his left hand. His right thumb and forefinger are cramped from 'rheumatism', his own diagnosis, for Charles has not seen a doctor in a very long time.

'Let me do that, Uncle,' I offer, taking the teapot from him to pour. He hands it over willingly and sits back in his armchair.

As we talk and munch biscuits, I try not to be moved by the small efforts he's made to spruce himself up. He's had a new haircut; the long wisps that once swirled up in the wind have been trimmed away. The yellow tie he's wearing is one I gave him last Christmas; the frayed collar of the pink shirt stands clear of his neck.

When I have filled him in on all that's been happening in Belfast, Charles says he wants to show me something. 'I haven't been entirely idle, you know,' he says, with a twinkle, replacing the cup on its saucer and pushing himself up from his chair. 'I have a few photos that may amuse you.'

With a glint in his eye, he retrieves an envelope and passes it over. 'Here, see if you recognize anyone in that.'

The photo on top of the pile, taken recently, shows my uncle in a full-length raspberry-coloured taffeta ball gown, worn over a white blouse, and topped with a mauve bonnet. Tight blonde curls cascade down his yet-to-be-inflated bosom. Red lips, rouged cheeks, blue eye-shadow and fake eyelashes complete the costume. Except for his hands, which hang skinnily by his sides, my uncle looks younger and healthier in drag. The annual staff play at St Columba's is one of the highlights of his year. By anyone's reckoning, he is a very experienced dame. The drawers of the cabinet behind us are stuffed with the scripts of pantomimes my grandmother used to write for our Church of Ireland parish to perform over New Year: her first, *The Enchanted Golfball* (starring the Ogey Bogey Fairy of the Nineteenth Hole), being her most distinctive contribution before she reverted to stock plots such as *Mother Goose*, filled with local gags. Throughout her seventies she took annual charge of the forty children, who were cast as rats or villagers, among whom I was often numbered, while my father, with a reluctance that equalled mine, played his own compositions on the piano. On stage, I huddled with the parish kids whom I barely knew, cringing with embarrassment and edging further and further into the wings. Charles, alone of the family, shared her enthusiasm and, as an Ugly Sister or Widow Twankey, always won the greatest applause.

As he leafs through the pictures, remarking happily on his colleagues' performances, I study him more closely. I cannot help but notice the things that do not matter much: the arm of his tortoiseshell glasses, mended with Sellotape; his suit jacket and V-neck jumper, spotted with food stains. More alarmingly, the red patches on his forehead and cheeks seem to have increased in size, while his nose seems more purple and swollen than ever.

My eyes stray to the black-and-white photograph framed on the wall, which shows a handsome young man carrying books under his arm. He is wearing a tie, V-neck jumper, tweed jacket, scarf, and a straw boater tilted back on his head, perhaps on the photographer's instruction. His smile is generous, his glance bashful and kind. My grandmother's visitors were usually surprised to learn this young man was Charles, taken while he was at Winchester; the picture, she would inform them proudly, had accompanied an article about English public schools in *Life* magazine. After Winchester, he had attended New College, Oxford, then taught at Eton, before returning to Tibradden in the mid-sixties. My father told me once that he thought the stress of teaching at Eton had prompted some sort of breakdown. 'My brother just lay on one sofa in the drawing room, while your grandmother lay on the other. They talked.' The memory clearly upset him so I asked no more. The part-time job teaching languages at St Columba's had put an end to this period, and the staff common room has served for years as a highly congenial home-from-home.

I hand the photos back. My uncle resumes slurping his tea. We have not yet discussed how Colin and I will share the house with him and I am not sure how much thought he has given to the subject. Years of living with his mother and Muriel have left him wary of fussing women.

'Uncle,' I begin, setting down my cup, 'have you had any ideas about how best we should organize things?'

'Well, yes, as you like, darling,' he replies quickly. He pushes back his armchair and, looking up at the ceiling, raises his voice a little as he used to for teaching. 'I've been chiefly thinking about your computers. I hope I have enough of our plugs.'

I try not to smile. There is only one modern square three-pin socket in the house, and that is in the dining room. The rest are the round sockets that were installed by my grandmother over the summer of 1939, as she waited to discover exactly when her husband would be called abroad to serve his regiment in the coming war. Whenever my uncle buys any new electrical item, he has to hunt for a round Bakelite plug among the defunct heaters, lamps and radios stored in the study and replace the new with the old. His stock of plugs is dwindling. When we've stayed in the past, we have tethered our lives to the twenty-first century via a long extension cable from the one dining-room socket. There is no washing-machine, no tumble-drier, no working dishwasher, no microwave and no shower. Indeed, there is no mains water supply, the tanks instead being filled by a gravity-fed system from the stream.

My uncle's ability to adapt his own needs to the gradual obsolescence of his environment is not one we can emulate. The lead wiring is a fire hazard. Blue sparks fly out from the socket in my old bedroom whenever I unplug the Hoover. My uncle's solution is just to shut the door on that room, as he has on several others. The house is still uninsured. His greatest fear is of overloading the circuit that is kept in delicate check by the ceramic fuses mounted high on the pantry wall.

It is clear my uncle cannot afford to rewire his house to suit our needs; nor should he be asked to do so. The solution I've come up with is to install new circuits with their own circuit-breakers in four rooms that Colin and I could adapt for our own use: the basement kitchen, the main bedroom, my grandfather's dressing room, and the den. In addition, we will turn the pantry into a safe and working galley kitchen to meet my uncle's very modest requirements. A microwave, I suggest, would transform his life.

At this my uncle shows his first sign of alarm. 'Oh, I don't think I need one of those,' he says. 'I get by with my little heater.'

'Trust me,' I tell him. 'They're not expensive.'

He listens patiently as I outline the gourmet alternatives to Fray Bentos steak and kidney pie.

'You can eat with us as well, whenever you like,' I tell him.

'Thank you, darling. That would be nice.'

'Is that all right, then, Uncle?' I ask, watching closely for any sign that I've overstepped the mark in proposing that Colin and I occupy four rooms. The kitchen and bedroom are museum exhibits of the days when they were inhabited by Muriel and my grandmother; in the den and dressing room, as in so many other rooms, the flotsam and jetsam of Charles's daily life have washed up along the high-water mark of his ancestors. I had anticipated that the job of sorting through these rooms would be at the forefront of his mind.

He bites his lip and frowns. Something is bothering him.

'Does Colin really want to use the den for a study?' he asks presently, doubtful that his former nursery could be an appealing place to work. 'It's a bit cold, and shabby. I doubt he will be very comfortable there.'

He pauses for a minute, trying to think of a fitting alternative. 'I could possibly begin on the study down here. That might suit him better.'

I am touched by the hospitality of this offer. The study is the masculine heart of the house. It's where my uncle files his papers laterally, on sofa, table, chair and floor. It is very difficult to traverse the room, never mind clear it. I assure him the den will do fine.

'Well, then,' says Charles, clearly relieved not to have to think any more about it. 'Let me know if you need any help.' He picks up *The Times* and returns to the crossword. I clear away the tea-things and wheel the trolley out, pulling the drawing-room door closed behind me. As I rattle off to the pantry, I catch what could be a glint of amusement in the crocodile's eye.

★

Late in the evening I search out the linen for my grandmother's bed, setting aside the candy-stripe flannelette to find the double sheets at the bottom of the hot press. There are two double beds in the room, one for my grandmother and one for Owen. 'He was very good to me,' Kitty would say. It had always been clear a husband could receive no higher accolade.

About a week ago, Charles told me, a jackdaw fell in through the chimney, and the evidence of its panicked flight from window to window is still apparent on the carpet and bedspreads. It had taken him some time, he said, to identify what the noise was, and where it was coming from, before discovering the bird perched on my grandmother's bedstead. After a full hour's chase, he had finally managed to throw a sheet over it and bundle the whole package out through the window. It had been quite exhausting. 'I'm afraid I haven't yet got round to cleaning it up,' he apologized.

I get a basin of water and Fairy Liquid, scrub the carpet and then begin remaking the beds. I throw the bedspread and blankets onto the floor and strip off the old sheets and under-blanket. All of a sudden, the memory of my grandmother's still body surprises me as I float the white cotton sheet, impeccably darned, out over the blue horsehair mattress. It must be eight years ago that she died. A boyfriend picked me up from the airport, but by the time I arrived the rector was already upstairs consoling Charles. It was Muriel who greeted me at the top of the stairs, and asked that I wait while she washed and clothed my grandmother in her best nightdress and laid her out beneath the eiderdown. I remember the grief and embarrassment of her embrace when she came to tell me I could go in now and sit with her if I wanted to, to pay my respects.

It seemed a long way across the room to my grandmother lying here in this bed. Her face was not calm, or asleep, as I'd been led to expect. It was more that her features held no expression at all. Her skin and hair and hands had become matter invested with no more importance than linen or leather or water. It seemed to me then that the body was just a vessel for the spirit. It seemed right to say her spirit had departed in peace from this place. God's will. I stroked her cheek as I would never have done when she was alive, and told her how glad I was that she was with Owen, as she had always believed would be her reward.

I finish making the bed and undress. The long evening's twilight has faded to darkness. The scent of old feathers and lavender talc promises an easy sleep. Through the open window I hear the stirring of the trees taking over from the rush of traffic on the M50. Colin will be here soon to share this with me, I think, wondering what he will make of the transition into this world of dust motes and the relics of my ancestors. I think our own story, four years in the making, should be light and steady enough to weather it. The thought of him shuttles across my mind, un-weaving the prospect of sleep.

I come down late the next morning. Charles is eating his egg in the dining room. He looks up from the article he has been squinting at, his glasses in his hand, and invites me to help myself to cereal, waving towards the packets stacked on the hotplate in the corner. I pour myself a bowl of cornflakes, look for the sugar and stop.

'Umm, Uncle, are these mouse droppings by any chance?' I ask.

He gets up quickly, and puts on his glasses the better to examine the small black crumbs as if he had never noticed them before. 'Hmm, yes. They do look like droppings, don't they? I'll have to get a trap down at Devine's.'

He returns to his egg. I pour myself a cup of tea, struggling to match his nonchalance, and sit down at the veneer table, which Charles bought recently to replace the mahogany original with the ball-and-claw foot I used to shine. It was stolen a few months ago: the thieves simply lifted the table out of the window while he stood helpless at the dining-room door. 'Bastards', he called them, when telling us of the robbery. It was the only occasion on which I'd ever heard my uncle swear. He had been made to feel ashamed of his own vulnerability and I felt ashamed that I had not been there to protect or comfort him.

After breakfast I begin to clear away. Spilt sugar and cornflakes are scattered over the blue cloth, which, judging from the wine stains, can't have been laundered since the Christmas party. Two packets of sliced pan, white and brown, lie open with the torn heel sticking out of one. The lip of the milk jug has a thick yellow crust built up over several mornings. I inspect the mantelpiece, and then the corner cabinet, and then the sideboard for mouse droppings. The mice have had a happy time.

As I wheel the trolley into the pantry, my heel catches on the underlay poking through the lino, like mould on a piece of bread. At some stage Muriel sensibly waterproofed the tops of the presses with sticky-back plastic, but now it's manky with grease and burn marks. I search for a cloth. Above the sink, a few bedraggled tea-towels are draped on a wire. The white iron drainer, bearing its chipped patent number, is flaking with rust and fully stacked with teacups and plates. I begin to put them away before I realize they will all have to be washed again. The sink is still full of yesterday's crockery. It seems my uncle considers a day-long soak in Fairy Liquid all that washing-up requires. This explains the taste of the tea. 'Well, what did you expect?' my mother says, when I call her. 'Your uncle and Kitty always had staff.'

There is nothing for it but to get busy. The morning passes

quickly. By the time Charles comes back from lunch at one of the local carveries, the stained-glass panels in the pantry door are gleaming, and there are two bin-bags full of old tins and bottles ready to go out in the rubbish. 'Don't exhaust yourself,' he tells me, casting a glance at the bags without any real under- standing of what's been achieved. He makes for the drawing room and settles into his armchair for an afternoon of watch- ing golf on television. In a little while, I join him and gaze at the immaculate green sward and blue skies that suggest a lumi- nous perfection is attainable elsewhere.

The Irish golfer is doing well. 'Did you know that he once wanted to buy this house?' my uncle says, without turning round from the screen. I didn't.

'Nice chap he was too. He stayed here for about an hour chatting. Oh, what a shot!'

The Irish golfer bends down and plucks his ball out of the hole with a smile. I wonder whether I want to know the answer to my next question.

'Were you at all tempted by his offer?' I ask, trying to keep my tone neutral.

Charles doesn't answer immediately. 'No, not really,' he says eventually. From the way he says it, I guess he gave the offer some consideration. Not necessarily on account of the money, but if he were to sell Tibradden to anyone, he would have enjoyed the new owner being this man.

'Of course,' my uncle continues from the depths of his chair, 'the whole place is worth a ludicrous amount of money.' He sighs. 'Letters come through the post offering staggering sums.'

I decide to risk a slightly different question, the harder one that was never quite broached at any of the meetings held in his accountant's office. 'Do you think you will ever need to sell?'

There's a long pause. 'No, I don't think so,' he replies, his voice more confident than the words might suggest. 'I sold a strip of land to neighbours last year and that should keep us going for a while.'

The television commentator notes that a new bunker has been added at the far side of the green. His tone is reverent. The mass of flowering shrubs suggests an army of gardeners stand ready to dead-head them for the cameras.

Aware of my silence, my uncle clears his throat and adds, 'And, well, you're here now.'

'Yes, I am,' I reply softly. I am not quite sure what he means by this, but he would appear to recognize my being here now as some sort of vote for the future. Whether I can build my life inside Charles's vision of the future, with no great alteration to the pattern of his days, I am less sure about. I want to thank him for holding out so mildly in his own life, so unassertively, that Colin and I can share it with him. At the same time, I am frustrated that these same qualities won't allow him to see himself as worthy of a little more reward. As I sit there with him, I pray my bossiness won't upset a relationship built on the discretion of our mutual care.

3.

July 2002

Over the summer, the great clearances begin. To tidy one room entails creating space in another for the mountain of paraphernalia deemed worthy of repair or re-use. Beneath a stack of suitcases in the den, we uncover an old valve radio with the capitals of Europe spelled out across its dial. Súgán chairs, their seats unravelled, nurse broken heaters in their skeletal crates. A square black case opens up to reveal a gramophone; the arm, out of its cradle, is poised to play a 78 of 'I Wore A Little Grey Bonnet', sung by Gertie Millar (soprano) with orchestral accompaniment. I discover my old cot, decorated with a transfer of Bambi, marooned beside a specimen cabinet containing glass cases of pinned butterflies, birds' eggs and tiny Chinese figures, which I take to be relics of the year my infant uncle spent in Shanghai. A sun-bleached poster proclaiming 'Come to the West Indies!' above a native figure dressed in a grass skirt and waving a pair of maracas reveals a shadow on the wall where one corner hangs down. Small boxes of artificially bright feathers and pheasant wings, all tangled together with nylon line, are piled on the deal table where Charles used to tie trout flies. I riffle through old parish newsletters, alumni gazettes, committee minutes of the Select Vestry and the Forces Help Society, black-and-white school photographs, my own discarded textbooks: some are boxed, the majority just dumped. Behind two broken armchairs I discover an entire bookcase of Folio Society volumes, including a richly illustrated set of *The Thousand and One Nights*, while a curtain behind the door conceals my father's complete run of *Astounding Science Fiction*.

My uncle seems unperturbed by the eviction of these ancestral effects from the corners of his house. I buy cardboard archive boxes and scrawl the nature of their contents in freezer marker on the side. Armfuls of paper are brought to the drawing room for Charles to sort through: I return to find boxes labelled 'Miscellaneous – some important' and stow these in the hall awaiting removal to some more permanent home.

Evidence of an earlier regime survives in the tall linen presses my grandmother installed on the landing. 'Side Board Cloths', 'Pillow Slips', 'Hand Towels' and 'Bolster Cases' read the labels, neatly written in Muriel's looped hand. They seem to have served as 'No Trespassing' signs to my uncle, for above them the stacks of linen are still neatly starched, each item ticked off in a laundry book. Several poultry registers, recording the number of eggs laid each day and the occasional death (9 September 1973: 'one bantam taken by dog fox') show a similarly methodical regard for household management. Under my grandmother's direction, as befitted a past president of the Girl Guides, everything found its proper place.

'It all comes from the army, I suppose,' says Colin, a little nervously, looking inside. We are standing in my grandfather's dressing room, where I used to sleep as a young child with the door open to Gran's bedroom so I could call her if I needed to. One item of furniture dominates the room: the plain brown Model YCH wardrobe, patented by Compactom with showrooms at 143 Regent Street, London W.1. It is designed for a gentleman with a valet. The heavy doors are open to reveal a series of glass compartments and cardboard files politely assigned to 'Soft Collars', 'Neckties', 'Dress Vests', 'Scarves and Wraps' and the mysterious 'Requisites'. A board at the bottom lifts up to reveal a discreet locker for 'Sundries'.

In the chest of drawers opposite, we find stiff white waist-coats and card dickies between layers of crinkly tissue. I lift up a waistcoat, still paper-sharp, and hold it up to the light. It is a little foxed in places and smells of biscuits. Matching dicky bows in dimpled poplin are neatly secured with a ribbon at the back of the drawer. With a tinge of regret for teenage Saturday nights when I plundered these clothes, I pack them all into suitcases and ring the wardrobe department of the Abbey Theatre. 'By all means, darling,' Charles said, when I suggested it. 'I simply haven't known what to do with them all.' He is surprised when I return home with a cheque made out in his name.

Peter, the electrician who is installing the new circuits, helps us lift the empty Compactom onto a piece of lino and slide it heavily into a corner of the main bedroom. Colin has his back to me as he unfolds his clothes from their piles on the floor and considers where to place them in this monument to masculinity. The mirror inside the door reveals a wry glance of satisfaction as he slips his parka onto a hanger and hooks it to the concertinaed rail labelled 'Tail Coats'.

'Come with me to Dublin,' I urged Colin four years ago, shortly after we first got together. 'We'll stay at Tibradden and you can meet my family and then decide if you still love me.'

Charles picked us up at the airport. I spotted him standing behind the barrier, dressed in a shapeless tweed overcoat and scarf, trying to smooth back the long wisps of hair that had been blown about by the wind. I waved and he reappeared from behind the crowd with a gleeful smile, flapping his arms in excitement.

We crammed our bags into his Opel Corsa. The seats were still white with the hair of Poppy, my grandmother's overweight Jack Russell that had died two years previously. Colin reluctantly sat in front. He had taken out his earring in the baggage hall, despite my insistence that Charles wouldn't notice it, never mind object to its presence.

The M50 required all my uncle's concentration so conversation was limited until we arrived at Tibradden. The house loomed out of the dark, big and gloomy. The two Massy ancestors, one either side of the hall, gazed superciliously down from their ornately carved and gilded frames. I could see Colin taking it all in and was glad when Charles ushered us into the drawing room for a sherry.

He had booked a table for us in the restaurant at Killakee stables, where he had enjoyed a decent supper a few weeks ago. 'I thought you might like to show Colin a little piece of family history,' he said: the weathervane at Killakee, perforated by his father's air rifle, was one of the stop-off points on his local tour.

After polite conversation, we excused ourselves to 'freshen up'. Colin wanted to iron a shirt, so I showed him the ironing-board in the den and left him to it while I hunted through the suitcase for makeup bag and hairbrush. 'It does work,' I'd assured him, plugging it in.

Our beginnings were complicated, but before leaving for Oxford I had told Charles the bare details. Colin was the only man I had ever met whom I could imagine marrying. He was my age and worked as a lecturer in Huddersfield. He had married young and had children aged four, six and ten, but he was no longer living with their mother. They had been talking for a while of separating formally, but meeting me had prompted the final decision. He was from Belfast, Dundonald to be precise.

Charles had listened intently. When I'd finished, I searched out his gaze. His expression was curiously mild. 'I see,' he had eventually said, 'and what is his name?' The sound of my voice announcing it shocked me. Some great step in our relationship seemed to have been taken.

My uncle had looked down at his hands clasped together in front of him so that the tips of his index fingers rested lightly on his lips. The room was very quiet for a time. We were both thinking about the children, whom I had yet to meet. In a carefully controlled voice, he had finally said that he believed Dundonald was where one of his colleagues visited her sister. I understood from this that Charles was prepared to accept whomever I decided to introduce as my partner on his own merits.

I had nearly finished dressing when I heard Colin call my name. I went out to the landing and discovered him at the door of the den, looking pale and shaky, his freshly ironed shirt held out at arm's length.

'My God, what happened?' I asked, leading him into the bedroom to sit down.

He didn't say anything for a few seconds, just put his fingers up to his head and started prodding around. 'Umm, could you check whether I've cut myself?'

On cue, a steady flow of blood began to trickle down his forehead. He had whacked his head off the corner of the mantelpiece when he stood up from unplugging the iron. There was an inch-long gash near his crown, which looked to me like it needed stitches.

We could hear Charles foostering about in the hall, humming to himself. 'Look,' said Colin, 'say nothing. I don't want to make a fuss after he's gone to so much trouble. Just give me five minutes and I'll get ready.' I could see he was unlikely to change his mind, however much I argued that we should go to have it checked out at Tallaght's A&E department. Two Panadol and some Savlon were all he would accept for now.

As we stepped out of the car at Killakee, the holes in the weathervane were clearly visible against the bright night sky. Colin looked up politely as Charles pointed it out, then staggered against the door. I took his arm and we proceeded inside.

'I told them you were a vegetarian,' Charles pronounced the word with great delicacy, 'and so I hope they have prepared something suitable.'

'Thank you. I'm sure whatever comes will be fine.'

Behind the menu, Colin discreetly dabbed at his wound with a balled-up handkerchief, attempting to stem the flow of blood above his hairline. Belatedly, it occurred to me he might be suffering from concussion. My uncle had yet to notice anything wrong. He was recounting for us the sad story of his great-grandfather Lord Massy, who had died a bankrupt alcoholic in the gate-lodge of his estate here at Killakee, when Colin excused himself and left the table.

'I think they've done things very well here,' Charles said, glancing around with approval at the blood-red carpet, the dark timbers and mahogany furniture. 'And I do like your friend.' He paused for a moment, then added, 'He seems to be very patient.'

A baked avocado was waiting by the time Colin returned from the bathroom. He was not looking well. At the sight of the bruised mush oozing through the goat's cheese crust, he blanched further but managed a compliment for Charles's ears. 'Do you want to go home?' I whispered, when the waitress came.

'No, I'm fine,' he shushed, and turned to ask Charles another heroic question about the bankrupt lord.

*

At the start of August, we hire a van to fetch our remaining belongings from Belfast. The summer has gone in a haze of dust and skips. The din of jackhammers reverberates through the house as plasterers hack mortar off the kitchen walls in the basement, in preparation for new coats of lime.

The work has revealed some of the house's prehistory. The window boards were once lower to the ground and have been raised with brick rubble. Charles rummages in the study bookcase and emerges with a map dated 1832, showing an L-shaped farmhouse belonging to a Mr John Jones on the present site. We spread it out in the kitchen and work out that the current house must have been built on the foundations of this earlier one, perhaps with the original entrance leading straight out of the back door to Mutton Lane. On Peter's advice, we prise off the two-ply nailed around the vast fireplace and discover behind it the granite lintel he had predicted. The stone is blackened by the fire that would have served as the flaming heart of the house, circulating hot water in kettles to all parts for all ends. I wonder when it was replaced by the range that was in turn replaced by the electric cooker when I was a young child. I feel like an archaeologist digging through the layers of other women's domesticity.

As a girl I used to open the door to the basement stairs and peer into the dark, hearing the roar of the boiler's furnace. 'May I come down?' I would call.

'Yes, come on, pet,' Kathleen's voice would rasp from the depths.

I would descend slowly, wary of the boiler that seemed always to shudder on the brink of explosion, before skipping to safety through the kitchen door. A pair of hands, smelling of stew and Capstan, closed over my eyes and I was held in against a body that felt soft and warm and familiar. 'Guess who?' teased a voice in my ear.

'Is it Muriel?' I'd hazard in our old routine.

'No.'

'Is it Ginger?' I'd guess again, with a giggle, Ginger being the cat that lived in the kitchen.

'Are you daft? Do these feel like paws?'

'It's Kathleen!' I'd cry triumphantly, earning my release and a pinch on the cheek.

Kathleen wore bright cardigans and flowered dresses over torn tights and slippers. She rarely left the kitchen, save on Sunday when my uncle drove her to mass in Ballyboden, though sometimes, when I was on my way to bed, I would listen to her low, hoarse tones on the telephone in the hall. Her bedroom, at the top of the kitchen stairs, was a no-go area, just as Muriel's was. I'd glimpse the pattern of the pink wallpaper through the open door but that was all.

Muriel used to watch us through creased and smiling eyes. She would chuckle at our routine, but she never participated and something about it made her uncomfortable. She and Kathleen each had their own armchair, either side of an oil-clothed table, on which the radio sat next to a stack of puzzle magazines and bags of knitting. This was where Ginger would lie, like a tattered Bagpuss, on his own cushion. 'So have you come to visit us, pet, or is it that old yoke only you're after?' Kathleen would ask, lifting me up to sit atop the pile of cushions on her chair so that I could reach the cat. She moved heavily around the kitchen while I chattered away, taking up an unravelling glove to move hot dishes in and out of the oven.

She used to talk a lot about her sister and her nephew, Tony, and his son, Stephen, who was about my age and who wanted then to join the guards. When they came to visit, Kathleen entertained them in her 'parlour'. This was actually a two-room flat located in one corner of the courtyard adjacent to the house. Valentine, the herd who'd been Muriel's uncle, had once lived there but now it was Kathleen's space alone, set aside for when she had company. Sometimes she'd invite me in to examine her collection of china carthorses, and to play with her cat, Buttons, who was kept in one of the outhouses. 'Kathleen's family are here today,' my grandmother would announce, 'so we're having a cold lunch.'

She died about four years ago and I, away in England, missed her funeral. The last time I saw her, she had moved to a council flat in Ballinteer. It was neat and warm with the gas fire on; trickles of condensation shone high up on the wall. 'I see you have the heavy horses still,' I said, pointing to them on the mantelpiece, hoping to remind her of the times we'd spent out in her parlour when she'd told me who had given each one to her, and what breed it was. But I couldn't cheer her that day. She told me how relieved she was to have moved out of the Whitechurch estate, where she'd been living since she had retired. It was a rough place, she said, although here was not much better. She'd had trouble with junkies; the word caused her to tremble with fear and indignation. She didn't like to go out because they'd been dealing on her doorstep and she was afraid. They hadn't been around as much since a few of the neighbours had confronted them, but still she worried at night.

'Will your uncle not come in?' she had asked eventually.

Charles's car was parked outside on the road, the wipers going, while he listened to the radio and waited for me to return. I had not been able to look at him as I got out of the car, bearing his gift of biscuits and tea-towels, so ashamed was I that he would not go in himself. 'He said to apologize, Kathleen, he has a cold and didn't want to pass it on to you.'

'Ah, well,' she looked down at her lap, 'you can give him my regards anyhow.'

We had driven back up the mountain in the usual way, Charles slowing to a crawl behind every cyclist and pedestrian, before revving suddenly in erratic bursts of courage to overtake them. He had turned the radio on and off the whole way home. 'Stop it,' I'd wanted to shout. 'Thirty years of cooking for you, and you can't show her the courtesy of visiting her in her own home.' But, as usual, I said nothing.

Sitting in her old kitchen now, the bare walls awaiting their first shell of plaster, I feel the thick dark pressing in through the bars on the window. At the top of the bank stands the yew hedge, planted when the house was built to conceal the basement from view. I wonder who needed this screen more: those who worked here or those who walked the path above? Whose privacy was it planted to protect? My elbows rest on the wooden beading Kathleen had nailed on to stop eggs rolling off onto the floor.

What was it that kept Charles in the car outside Kathleen's house? He has always been charitable, and has conscientiously kept up a correspondence with Muriel, although he says that her letters merely approve whatever news he tells her of his own. She retired to live with her brother on the family farm outside Birr, and then, when her brother died, she bought a cottage in nearby Rathcabban with her sister, Ethel. Charles visited them last summer and was pleased to find them well looked after, with good neighbours and a carer sent by the Health Service. Perhaps the difference lay in the fact that he and Muriel shared a parish whereas he and Kathleen did not. Every Sunday he used to drop Kathleen to mass at the Augustinians in Ballyboden before returning to collect the rest of the household for the service at Whitechurch. He was not in any sense anti-Catholic; it was just that he and Muriel observed the same Church of Ireland calendar of harvest suppers and sales of work and thus belonged to the one community outside the house. She attended the Mothers' Union and gleaned there bits of parish news, which she enjoyed passing on to Gran and Uncle ahead of anyone else. Kathleen had her separate faith, her separate life. But I think the main reason Charles stayed in the car that afternoon was that he could not face Kathleen's loneliness when he had so long faced away from his own.

As the summer closes and the evenings darken, I often find Colin and Charles in the drawing room, reading beside their respective lamps, Charles in his armchair, Colin on the sofa. It could be an Oxford common room. Very occasionally, I feel the lack of a tea trolley to wheel before me. On one of his regular visits to Charles, the rector, Horace, took me aside. 'Forget all you know about your uncle and just think about his character and who he is. What should he have been, do you think, if he could start his life over again?'

'I don't know,' I answered, a little frustrated by the question. 'A father, I think.'

'Yes, of course,' Horace agreed patiently, 'but I really intended the question professionally.' He paused to watch my bewilderment for a moment before going on to suggest that from his own knowledge of the man, on committees and personally, Charles would have made a superb don.

It was not the place or time to suggest that the ways of Oxford dons might have moved on significantly from the model Horace had in mind. His point was well made. I never heard Charles himself voice such an ambition. He still read the literature he had studied for his degree in modern languages at New College; he still delighted in etymology, an interest that had gained him work, when he graduated, compiling *Cassell's Dictionary of Modern French*. He had never betrayed to me any sense of disappointment in his life: National Service, a few unhappy years teaching at Eton, and then the return to St Columba's and Tibradden. As the eldest son, he must have known that the property would become his responsibility on his father's death; as a bachelor he might also have expected to become carer and companion to his widowed mother. England had provided him an elsewhere, a short time in the sun as the shadow cast by the house lengthened, but an elsewhere in which it would have been foolish to believe for long.

The midges are out, bobbing above the rhododendrons outside the window. Positioned once more behind a book in my grandmother's armchair, I surreptitiously glance across at the two men on the sofa. Colin's glasses are perched on the end of his nose, his right leg crossed over his left in unconscious imitation of his companion. He is listening closely as Charles explains how to unscramble a clue from the cryptic crossword in today's *Irish Times*. 'Here's one that's appropriate,' Charles says, jabbing the paper with his biro. 'Four down, six letters: "The relatively little subject that this has".' The big red *Chambers* lies open on the floor beside them, an abandoned copy of Colin's book, *Deconstructing Ireland*, beside it. Earlier in the day, I had been passing the door and had heard Charles mutter in lexicographical disgust – '*Aporetic*, bah!' – as he snapped the dictionary shut. From this, I had surmised correctly that he was once again engaged in the battle to read Colin's monograph. 'The "relatively little subject",' Colin murmurs. 'I suppose I need to think of relations, do I?'

Charles nods, then adds another hint. 'What article indicates a subject?'

Colin looks quizzical. His determination not to lose face over a crossword puzzle amuses me. I raise my own book

47

higher. The verdurous call of pigeons dissipates the silence as he scribbles abbreviated relatives on a small scrap of paper. 'Oh, I get it,' comes the sudden sound of triumph from the sofa. 'It's "thesis" – "the sis" – isn't it?' They look touchingly pleased with each other as Charles writes in the letters and their heads bow again.

4.

One bright Tuesday morning, a large silver Mercedes pulls up in front of the house. The smartly dressed driver takes out a briefcase and a roll of papers, then reaches in to unpeg his jacket from the hook behind the front seat before walking around the car to admire the view.

He greets me with a professional smile and asks whether he can speak to the owner of the house. 'It's just about the new County Development Plan,' he says. The council have engaged his firm of consultants to assess local opinion of the current zoning in our area.

I take the proffered business card and usher the visitor into the dining room, before fetching Charles from his paper. The word 'consultant' prompts a low groan. 'What do these people want?' he asks, flinging the paper down impatiently. 'You had better ask Colin to come and sit in with us in case there's some jargon I don't understand.'

In the dining room, we find the consultant still standing politely. 'Would you mind if my niece and her fiancé stay for the meeting?' Charles asks.

'Not at all, whatever you wish,' the man replies. Setting down his briefcase, he peels an elastic band off the roll of maps from under his arm. With all the razzmatazz of a carpet-seller in the Istanbul bazaar, he unfurls a map of Dun Laoghaire/Rathdown across the table and smooths it out, matter-of-factly accepting the jug and salt cellar I offer him to weight the corners.

We gather round the map. Beyond the orbital route of the M50, the outer suburbs of Dublin brim against the hills in little splashes of cul-de-sacs. The consultant waits till we've located ourselves, then lurches forward with his pencil.

'This shows the current plan,' he says. 'This area here is still zoned agricultural.' His pencil hovers above Tibradden Road. The county boundary traces the twists and bends of our old estate wall, before leaving the road at the bend below Rockbrook and tracking cross-country up Tibradden Mountain and on to Glencullen. On the city side of the road, the fields are white: they are under the authority of neighbouring South Dublin council, so their zoning need not be shown on this map. The fields on the hillside, including our own, are shaded mint green to designate 'Zone B', which, the key explains, is for 'rural amenity and the promotion of agriculture'.

'Generally,' he says, 'the planners don't permit development above the line of the M50, but with each new plan, all the county zonings have to be looked at again.'

He waits while Colin and I examine the map more closely.

'I noticed the livestock out the front here on my way in, so I presume you still farm?' he asks, turning to face Charles for the first time.

'Yes,' says my uncle, with an air of slight chagrin. 'We keep a few cattle and sheep.'

'You've a terrific view,' he says. 'Have your family lived here long?'

Colin looks sideways at me. The consultant's attempts at small-talk are making us all a little uneasy. Colin asks him whether he'd mind explaining his purpose here today in a little more detail.

The man explains that the planners want to find out whether the current zonings accurately reflect the predominant activities in each area. This information will feed into a consultative process during which residents will have the chance to contribute to the development of the new county plan. For the purpose of this exercise, he simply needs to know whether my uncle intends to continue farming his land for the foreseeable future.

The crease in Charles's brow deepens as he searches for a polite way to evade a question he has successfully avoided for quite some time. The future of the farm is something we never talk about.

'Uncle,' I interpose, eyeing the consultant, 'I think we can safely say, can't we, that you intend to go on farming for now?'

'Yes, that would be right,' Charles confirms, with some relief. 'You see, the farm is run by an elderly couple and I really don't know what else they would do. It wouldn't be fair to disturb their livelihood, you understand.'

'Do they live in the gate-lodge I passed on the way in?'

'Yes,' I answer. Charles is looking alarmed now.

'I see,' says the consultant, taking in our hesitation. 'So am I right to say that, for your purposes then, it would suit if this area retained its agricultural zoning?'

'I suppose so,' I agree, looking questioningly at my uncle.

He nods. 'Yes, that's right,' he says again. I can see he is still trying to work out what all these questions are for.

The visitor looks around him, appraising the holes in the rug and the tattered curtains. 'This must be a lovely house to live in,' he says, in a tone that suggests it mightn't be. 'Might I ask how old it is?' Charles tells him. 'And are all these people family members?' He gazes admiringly at the gilt-framed portrait of Mrs White, a Victorian lady in a black dress with ample *décolletage*, who is so badly painted that her right arm appears to be detached from its shoulder.

'Yes,' replies Charles, 'in one way or another.'

The consultant extracts a second map, more local still, and

lays it over the map of the county. Three Rock Mountain inter-cedes between our valley and the purple fields of Carrickmines, which appear to have been unzipped for development by the future path of the motorway. A string of perspiring dashes indicates the Wicklow Way as it climbs up towards the masts on Three Rock's summit. They are depicted here as small nee-dles pinned at the junction of two sets of contour levels, as if the Ordnance Survey had employed an acupuncturist to palli-ate the mountain landscape by rebalancing its gradient. I fancy that the paleness of the green of our fields suggests an official lack of conviction about Zone B, or even outright scepticism that agriculture is an activity worth 'promoting' in this area.

The consultant is addressing Charles in conciliatory tones. It appears the house and gate-lodge have been included on the list of protected structures, which is why they stand out as tiny blocks of flamingo pink among the black blocks of our neigh-bours' houses. There was an appeals process, the consultant is saying, but he thinks the deadline has passed. In any case, the listing could prove more of a help than a hindrance, allowing us to apply for grants to support what he terms our 'conserva-tion project'.

'In the end, I don't think there will be any changes to the zoning up around here,' the visitor assures us, rolling up his maps and snapping them tight with the rubber band. As Colin and I stand in the doorway shaking hands, he drops his voice to address me alone.

'There is just one thing, though, I should mention. On the way in I couldn't help notice the PVC sun-porch at the front of your gate-lodge.' He leans in a little. 'Look, it's beyond my remit, but if the lodge is listed, that really should come down. It's the sort of addition that might be subject to an enforce-ment order. Sometimes it's better to pre-empt the planners, keep on their good side, you know?'

Charles has overheard him. Rising from his chair, my uncle declares loudly: 'Please don't take that down!' He is visibly struggling to compose himself.

I step forward to comfort him, but feel Colin's hand on my arm. 'Let him speak,' he whispers.

'You must understand that an old woman and her Down's syndrome son live there and they built that porch with their own money. Sitting there in the sun is the one bit of recreation they share.' He is trembling with dismay. He takes a deep gulp of breath, and says, 'You mustn't take that down. I simply couldn't bear it.'

The pathos of his appeal freezes us all for a moment. 'It's all right, Uncle,' I say. 'I'm sure no one will upset the Kirwans.'

Our visitor has the good grace to look mortified. He apologizes and begins to explain again the limitations of his role here today. But Colin, with one look at Charles, who is leaning heavily on the table, ushers our visitor firmly out to the hall. I hear them talking in hushed tones on the steps before the car door bangs, and the emissary of modern times vanishes down the drive. Charles retreats to the drawing room, Colin to the den, and I sit for some time at the dining-room table, staring at nothing.

The visit seems to have exposed us all. Any time I have asked Charles, even in the most general terms, about what happens on the farm, he looks so pained I drop the subject. His accountant once confided to me that Charles had failed to record a farm profit for as long as he'd been doing the returns. It worries me that, all this time, its losses have been subsidized out of my uncle's own modest salary as a part-time teacher and the erratic dividend income that constitutes his pension.

I suspect that what our visitor today really wanted to find out was whether our fields have already been sold to a developer or whether they are still functioning as an active farm. The crowded maps make clear that our mint-green fields are among the last in the vicinity of the M50 that are still grazed. In Loughlinstown, Rathmichael, Carrickmines, Ballyogan, Stepaside, Sandyford, Ticknock, all the way round through Ballycullen, any remaining farmland has been re-zoned in shades of brown and black and grey. Recently I passed a sign on the N7 near Newcastle advertising an 'extensive land-bank' for sale. Beyond the sign lay a vast tillage field, its brown earth still bristling with yellow stubble. When, I wondered, did the term 'land-bank' come to substitute for 'property'? Driving on, I felt a sense of vertigo as if the landscape on either side of me were dissolving into liquid figures on a screen.

The meetings about Tibradden's succession have taught me enough about inheritance tax to know that the rise in land values would proportionately increase the bill levied on Charles's estate after his death. If Tibradden's one hundred and sixty acres were re-zoned for housing, the Revenue's bill could be met only by selling part of the farm. Whether this would leave the remaining acres a viable agricultural enterprise is something I don't know enough about farm economics to judge. Nor do I know whether Charles will leave the farm to me, or my brother, or my father, or to none of us at all. So many questions hang in the air, jostling for answers that Charles does not have the heart to find.

On Friday mornings, Joe Kirwan drives his wife Susie up the avenue from the gate-lodge at a quarter past ten to collect the wages. He comes round to the passenger side and hauls Susie out and up the steps to Charles's waiting arm. My uncle assists her in, a courtier to her queen, and stands in the hall to wait for the opening sally that has remained the same, regardless of the weather, for at least thirty years: 'I have never seen the like of it, Master Charles, so I haven't.' And my uncle choruses, as he always has, that the cold or wind or rain or sun is unsurpassed in its current violence. This ritual greeting satisfied, they disappear into the dining room.

Susie's strident imprecations against the escalating cost of contractors and feed, and the poor harvests of silage and winter oats, resound from behind the closed door. She, too, has seen a falling-off from past times when twelve or more men were under her command to clear ditches, lay hedges, shear sheep, calve heifers, harvest grain and attend to all the other tasks around the farm. When, unusually for a young woman in the mid-1950s, she inherited the position of steward or farm manager from her father, Mr Sheane, she was given great sway on account of her loyalty and intelligence. She was then thirty-one years old and had ideas of her own about how things should be done. There were murmurs that the men hadn't liked receiving orders from young Susie Sheane, but she had the full trust and support of my grandfather, Owen, who admired her force of character. A contemporary of Susie's told me that John Ballasty, my great-grandfather's tall, blond English driver, had once thrown a bucket of water over her when she wouldn't stop criticizing the way he was washing the car. She reported the incident, and my grandfather apparently gave Ballasty his marching orders there and then. Susie would even try to boss the indoor staff if they'd let her, I was told, and what they did was none of her business.

Eighty years old and nearly blind, Susie now resembles an Old Testament prophet not just in appearance – her heavy black coat, white hair, milky eyes – but in manner. She takes a keen interest in the births, marriages and deaths of the area, particularly the deaths. Charles has a theory that this natural morbidity stems from her father's faith. Mr Sheane's family came from Avoca, a regular Wicklow stop-over for proselytizing preachers, John Wesley among them. Although Susie's father was nominally a Church of Ireland member, and was buried from Whitechurch, according to his widow's faith, his people came from Methodist stock. Charles once told me that Mr Sheane himself had joined the Plymouth Brethren, a nonconformist sect that originated around the Powerscourt estate in north County Wicklow in the early nineteenth century. As a child, Susie would have been taught to seek personal salvation from a wrathful God, and to keep herself separate from the sinners of the world. Her upbringing, Charles implied, had left little room for doubt or error.

According to Charles, Susie has not set foot inside a church of any denomination since her son Joseph's birth. When she went into labour at the age of forty-six, she attributed the pains to a burst ulcer, unaware that she was pregnant, or so the story went. The shock and distress of the birth were compounded by her baby's disability. Susie and Joe were only recently married. Until then, Joe had been living in a bungalow less than a mile away at Cruagh with his mother and stepfather, and working in the forestry service, felling timber and planting trees high up on the mountain.

Her loyalty and her dependence, combined with her strength of character, have effectively deterred my uncle from ever broaching the subject of retirement. It is Susie who orders all the feed and supplies over the black Bakelite phone in our hall, which she views as her office line, her strong voice carrying to all corners of the house. It is Susie who still fills in forms for the Department of Agriculture, squinting hard at her own wavering hand. For years, Joe has managed the work of several men in the field and farmyard, with contractors hired in only to help with machinery tasks at harvest time. He paces himself at the heavier jobs – shearing, fencing, dehorning cattle, hard physical work for any man of seventy-four, never mind a man barely over five feet tall with the build of a wren. Joseph is seldom seen outside the lodge except on Fridays, when he waits in the car, playing with twine, before his parents take him shopping. In the meantime, the hedges grow leggy, the fields are spun out.

Joe and I meet in the scullery most mornings when he comes to deliver the milk in a pail. We have only the one milk cow, a big Friesian that walks herself up to the gate at daybreak awaiting the small, dark figure of Joe to emerge from the laurels. Each night before bed I set out the big creamery bowl on the drainer, a perforated metal disc to clamp the filter paper in place at the bottom of the steel strainer inside. Standing at the kettle the next morning, I find I am listening out for the trudge of gumboots on gravel, waiting to see Joe's white sheepdog, Moss, and Lassie, the Wicklow collie, gambol ahead of their master and down the kitchen steps, before he ducks down to look for me through the window and wave. Our chat in the scullery has come to seem an important part of my day. He lifts the pail and, picking out any blades of grass, pours the thick shiny milk into the bowl. He sets the bowl to stand on the zinc table behind him, and while he rinses out the pail I ask him questions about the small bits and pieces of agricultural news I've been gathering from the papers, so that he can tell me how things are done. Slag lime, he says, used to be a great thing for sweetening the grass, but with the factories gone you wouldn't get it now. Put a drop or two of cod-liver oil in the bottle for pet lambs if you want them to thrive.

We have always got on well, Joe and I. His memory is the best map of Tibradden, not just of its wells and our gravity-fed water supply, but of where I might find the last clump of white violets my great-grandfather used to wear in his buttonhole. 'But that's the way of it' is the phrase that recurs, suggesting, without criticism, a shared awareness of what else might be done, given the money and labour we both know aren't available. With Colin away in Belfast most of the week during term, and Charles asleep in bed, the scullery in the mornings has become a side-chapel where Joe and I prepare side by side for the lone tasks in the hours ahead.

The big Turkish oak in the Lawn is split in two by a November storm and one half topples down. The wood won't burn, says Joe, and he raps the trunk to show me it's hard as concrete. We look up uneasily at the half left standing and wonder aloud whether it will survive until April, when Colin and I are getting married here at Tibradden. 'It'll probably be standing long after I'm gone,' he assures me. Why I put any faith in this verdict, I don't know. One day last summer, I looked out of Colin's study window to see flames leaping high above the back wall of the walled garden. When I ran down the drive to investigate, I found Joe in his shirt-sleeves, tossing sticks of elder enthusiastically to the blaze. A small drum of petrol stood evidentially under a nearby cedar. 'What are you doing?' I raged at him, pointing to the big tank of kerosene not twenty yards away against the wall of his own house. He seemed amused by my distress. 'The wind is blowing the other way,' he explained calmly. 'You can only rid elder by burning it.' I noticed the scraps of silage wrap caught in the branches. I knew it was illegal to burn farm plastics, but it was too late to intervene.

By the start of December, the lime-plastering of the kitchen walls is finished. The putty colour fades to manila and the plasterers take down their halogen lamps and go. A fortnight later, Colin notices that a large area by the sink has crazed like an egg shell. Our electrician, Peter, taps around the walls with his fingernail. 'I wouldn't mind that,' he says, 'the key is good. Just don't put a nail in it.' Colin and I finish whitewashing the entire room with casein distemper at three o'clock on Christmas morning. We stand back, startled by the light reflecting off it, bright as a Bethlehem star.

A couple of months before our wedding, I'm sitting in what was my grandfather's dressing room, feeling pleased with my new study. A bookcase of poetry stands where the Compactom wardrobe used to be. I have set up the desk I bought years ago in Rathmines market, its surface still ringed from the mugs of tea that fuelled nocturnal hours before essay deadlines. I have sanded the floorboards and painted them an impractical cream. The walls were once hung with plain tobacco paper and decorated with black-and-white photographs of great-coated generals inspecting their troop ships. They are now papered bridally pale. The two arched windows are rouged with scarlet curtains and pelmet. Five deer bounce into view, including a grey-brown stag with five points to its antlers, which stops in front of the lime tree and turns seigneurially to face me.

This morning's task is to make a list of the poems I'm including in the anthology of new Irish poetry I've been commissioned to deliver by the end of the year. My reading is interrupted by a gunshot, which sounds close to the house. I go to the window. The sheep are bolting across the Lawn, with four deer bounding after them. I hurry outside. When I reach the bend in the drive, I see the fifth deer not ten yards inside the fence, trying in vain to get up. It is a young buck, its two horns still covered with soft fawn velvet. I climb into the field and approach the animal, crooning to try to calm it, or myself, down. Carefully, I catch hold of it and fold its body to the ground. Its head strains back against my grasp, revealing a small, precise hole, about a centimetre across, deep in its chest. What shocks me is not so much the fact of the deer being shot, as knowing a stranger feels free to discharge a loaded rifle within sixty yards of the house.

'Come out, you bastard, and get your venison,' I call into the bushes. There is no reply. Two wood pigeons start up with a clatter from the holm oak where they must have resettled. Either the hunter is hiding among the trees in front of me and will turn to leave through the farmyard, or else he is hiding in the thicket behind me, across the drive. I stand over the prostrate deer, whose long sides are heaving with the thirst for air. I feel stupid.

Joe will know what to do. Leaving the deer, I climb back out over the fence and call to the lodge. Susie says she thinks Joe might be up in the Green Gardens checking his own sheep; she promises to tell him I'm looking for him when he comes in for his tea. In the absence of a better plan, I decide to drive around the area to see if I can find any sign of the hunter's car. A boy waiting outside a neighbour's house says he hasn't seen anyone and neither have two others; all seem startled by my wide-eyed appearance. The question of what I will do if I find him, or them, scrabbles for a place among the expletives in my mind. It may not be the wisest thing, I hear some small voice argue, to take on a man with a loaded rifle. Nonetheless I drive down along Tibradden Road, faster than I should, and around to Rockbrook, but it must now be twenty-five minutes at least since the shot was fired, and there are no cars about.

I park on the drive and climb over the fence again. The deer looks to be lying still. I bend down and cup my fingers round its muzzle to feel for breath, but there is none. I am relieved it is dead. I pick it up by the hind legs and start to drag it heavily across the grass, uncomfortably aware that someone might be watching me still.

At the fence, I hear the welcome noise of a tractor coming

up the drive. Joe turns off the engine and climbs down. Together we heave the dead animal over the wire.

'The man that shot this lad here,' he says, lifting its head up gently, 'knew what he was after. He's caught it clean in the heart.'

The daylight has nearly gone, and the headlamps of the tractor light up Joe's face. He, too, is worried by the proximity of the shot. Either someone walked up the drive with a loaded rifle in the broad afternoon and shot the animal over the fence, or he shot up the field towards the drive. The bullets, Joe is telling me now, can travel for nearly a mile. Joe could have been out in the field, Charles or I could have been walking up the drive. The hunter took aim regardless.

Joe has reason to be afraid. A little over a year ago now, as Susie was getting Joseph ready to go down to Superquinn after collecting the wages one Friday morning, there was a knock at the front door. When Joe went to answer it, two tinker women, by his account, pushed past him, shutting the living-room door behind them while a third pinned Joe in the small entry. In the main room, the women demanded Susie's handbag, and when she refused they knocked her to the ground, kicked her and beat her, and made off with it anyway. The intruders exited casually, as if to leave the threat hanging that they could come again any time they liked. Joe mounted a security light above the front door, which now flashes on and off with every movement in the trees around.

'Come on, Joe,' I say, as the fear closes in on us, 'you must know how to bleed a deer.'

He looks at me twice to see if I'm serious. I can't tell whether I am or not. I feel giddy. The buck has been killed for venison, so why not give it a go? Using the loader and a length of rope fetched from the tractor, we manage with some effort to string the animal up from a sturdy branch of one of the cedars. If we can get it hanging and bleed it before the light goes entirely, I can then seek further instruction from a neighbour whose brother, Joe says, is a licensed deer-stalker. With any luck, my neighbour might be persuaded to prepare the carcass in exchange for half the meat, leaving us with enough to dish up to our guests in a few weeks' time. A young hart upon a mountain of spices to follow a reading from the Song of Solomon – what better feast for a wedding?

I stretch the neck taut so that Joe can slit the jugular with his pocket knife. The blood oozes sluggishly from the new wound, where I'd imagined a gush. I'm not sure now that we shouldn't have disembowelled the creature before stringing it up. I can remember eating game only once, when my grandmother was given a brace of pheasants by friends of Joe who shoot in the fields beyond the Ladies' Meadows. She stood in the pantry with her apron on, grimacing hard as she bound the claws together with garden twine and trussed the two birds up, entire as far as I remember, head-first above the sink. Their eyes, shrivelled like raisins, spoiled the glory of their feathers and I avoided going in for as long as they hung there.

The job done for now, Joe climbs back into his tractor and throws it into gear with all the eagerness of someone who has a good story to tell. I return to the house and call our neighbour for advice. 'What have you done with it so far?' he asks. Bleeding, it transpires, is only the start. Unless the spleen and lymph nodes are removed immediately, the meat will taint. It can be tricky enough to identify these organs, he says, even when you know what you're doing. After that, you take the belly out, then skin the deer and remove the head. I'll need a good saw or a very sharp knife for this last task. 'Are you sure you want to do this?' he asks me, several times. I admit I'm losing heart. It is now dark and beginning to rain. I really can't see Joe and myself managing to butcher this animal with any confidence, and I'm beginning to realize that my neighbour is simply not that desperate for venison casserole. In any case, he concludes, letting me off the hook, I've probably left it too long to rescue the meat. His advice is to bury the carcass or leave it for the foxes. I thank him and hang up, feeling queasy.

The vague sense that there is something else I'm meant to be doing crossed my mind at the thought of casserole. I check my watch. It is a quarter past six. It is Wednesday. With a warm rush of horror I remember that two ladies were due at six to discuss the catering requirements for our wedding reception. Any moment now, they will drive through our entrance, creep past the broken fence and the half-derelict gate-lodge with its flashing security light, on under the twin line of cedars, and be greeted by the sight of a deer, its throat slit, hanging by its hind legs from the last tree at the bend.

In a panic immeasurably more intense than that of two hours ago, I run back down the drive to the lodge. I find Joe in the tractor shed. I explain all. With a sigh, he climbs back in and reverses out again. The deer hangs darkly against the city's glow. Once again Joe takes his knife off his belt and, leaning out, begins to saw through his own good knots, while I steady the deer in my arms, keeping my eyes on the gate for the caterers' car.

The sudden weight causes me to stagger. One of the hind hoofs catches me across the face as the deer slithers head-first onto the grass. 'What should we do with it now?' I ask Joe. He gestures towards the thicket and, grabbing two legs each, we drag the carcass off deep into the rhododendrons. As I wipe my face on my sleeve, a set of headlights flashes in the gate and wobbles uncertainly towards us. I am about to step forward and wave when I reconsider. No need yet to identify myself. Ignorant of all that's gone on, at the sound of the doorbell Charles will rise from his armchair and usher them into the drawing room before he comes to look for me.

Even in the daylight, I'd find it hard to read the expression on Joe's face. He seems to have withdrawn into himself once more. 'You go on, Selina,' he says to me, turning to mount his tractor again. 'I'll dig a hole for it tomorrow.' We can hear the sound of car doors closing. There is no time now to apologize properly, so I thank him and hurry up the drive, feeling guilty.

5.

On the eve of the wedding, Mum arrives with her mother and
sister to take charge of the flowers. My aunt has brought pro-
teas, carried on her lap all the way from Cape Town where she
was on holiday. My grandmother has brought blocks of oasis
and small knots of wire. I find secateurs and a knife for my
mother, who moves among the foliage cluttering the kitchen,
picking out the longest stems for her vases in the drawing
room. She has stationed my grandmother at the head of the
table. Her hearing aid is switched off, so she remains oblivious
to her daughters' requests to pass them things as she works on
the centrepieces, pushing the stems in with surprising strength.
An air of repressed competition, not seen since the days of the
annual Dun Laoghaire Horticultural Show, resurfaces in the
house.

As the rain pours down, I gather Colin's daughters, Mel and
Jo, to raid the wet bushes for more rhododendrons. We have
umbrellas and coats and buckets, and Kitty's long basket to trip
over amid all the flowers. Lime-green umbellifers shed their
drops over us as we pluck and pull flowers with abandon.
'Don't we have enough now?' Jo asks eventually, and I have no
option but to return to the house, which is full of people who,
with the best of intentions, keep asking me to tell them where
things are.

In the late afternoon, my father and stepmother take me to
their house and feed me dinner and send me to bed as if I were

sixteen. In the early hours of the morning, I get up and go outside to sit on the back step and try to still the world from
whirring. A cat darts out through the railings and over the wall
into next door's garden. The night seems suspended in an
interval between noises; the terraces and streets beyond
breathe in a static rhythm of their own. I stay out, watching
the drizzle, until the back walls of the houses on the other side
of the convent field begin to sharpen in the rising light.

At the service in Whitechurch, Charles reads from the Sermon
on the Mount and makes of it a personal instruction from the
mild; the city on the hill standing before the congregation. Sitting beside us at the altar, the children have politely suspended
their scepticism and bow their heads when instructed in prayer.
Gratitude – for the generosity they have shown me as their
family has realigned in ways they could never have predicted,
and could scarcely have wanted – makes me vigilant on their
behalf. Seamus slouches into the suit trousers in which he feels
so ill-at-ease; Mel resists giving her skirt another tug, feeling
shy and exposed up here, while Jo, always eager for new experience and, at fifteen, at the right age to seek it out, takes it all in
and shines with her own light.

There are drinks and then dinner, interrupted by long
speeches, which my grandmother complains loudly are inaudi-
ble. Joe Kirwan, brilliantined and resplendent in the Louis
Copeland suit he had made for the occasion, gets merrily
drunk. Muriel, now in a wheelchair and accompanied by her
sister Ethel, watches all with her usual twinkle, and beams at
Joe as he tells me with great seriousness that today is the best
day of his life before he sways off, shepherded by my father-in-
law.

It is Charles who seeks me out for one of the first dances. To
whatever salsa rhythm the band is playing, we flap around in

some freestyle version of the Lambeth Walk. We are good together at comic turns. Around midnight, I look into the drawing room and see that he has resumed his armchair and is enjoying the company of five young women, who are seated around him, chatting freely to each other with the occasional nod to their host. He has shed his bow-tie and loosened his collar, and his hair is dishevelled, as befits a man who has just remembered how to party.

Seamus wilts at about two o'clock, and goes off with his cousins and grandmother to their B&B, but Jo and Mel stay up, the younger agog as she gulps a pint of Coke and watches the adults on the dance floor. The guests have clubbed together and paid off the coach driver to come back later. At sunrise he returns, an oddly classical figure in his sober uniform, to call time on the festivities. The party-goers walk down the drive, sandals and bags dangling from female arms. As the coach disappears down the lane, birdsong crystallizes in the frosty air. We turn back towards the house, Mel's head lolling against her father's shoulder, her sister's arm threaded through mine. Later today we will part again, the children bound for their mother's house while Colin and I depart for Peru. As our breath condenses together in the cold dawn, it seems possible to believe that the word 'stepmother' might come, in time, to be imbued with love.

A few weeks before the wedding, Charles finally admitted what had been obvious to everyone else for so long: that his persistent cough was getting no better.

On that particular morning, I was short of sleep, having been woken at dawn by the sound of protracted retching, terminating in a long yowl of pain from the bathroom. While lying in bed I decided that I had prevaricated long enough; the only way to get Charles to the doctor would be to emotionally blackmail him. 'You can't put this off any longer,' I said at breakfast. 'I'm not having you sick for our wedding.' The surgery made an appointment for the following week and, to my surprise, my uncle asked if I would accompany him.

Dr Khourie showed us straight in. Charles undressed, struggling to unfasten his cuffs, while I looked away, unsure whether to offer help or not. With the stethoscope in place he breathed in deeply as instructed, but at once a fit of coughing racked his body in deep shudders he struggled to control. As the fit subsided, and Charles wheezed in as best he could, I was alarmed to see the doctor's expression darken.

'How long have you had that cough?' he asked, letting the stethoscope drop from his ears.

'Oh, it comes and goes a bit,' replied Charles.

'And the lump on your forehead and these flushed areas around your face, have they been present for long?'

'For a few years,' he answered uncomfortably.

As I watched him getting dressed, I remembered my grandmother rubbing Vicks into his crooked fingers from the navy jar, reiterating the same firm words over again: 'It's no use, Charles, you'll just have to put up with a bit of fuss.' He had tolerated this nightly ritual in the knowledge, he told me once, that it was important for his mother to feel useful. My own mother had been advised by her Methodist grandmother, before agreeing to marry Charles's brother, to check under Charles's bed for whiskey bottles on account of his red nose. At St Columba's he'd acquired the obvious nickname 'Rudolph' long before I arrived there. In short, he had tolerated his flushed coloration for many years. The only reason he was here now was to appease me.

At a loss to understand why he refused to go for a check-up, I recently consulted a friend of his, hoping she might advise a better course of action than the emotional blackmail

I proposed. She sympathized with my frustration but pointed out that what appeared to me to be self-neglect was better understood as a form of stoicism born in a post-war age of austerity – difficult to live with, but admirable nonetheless. Charles's was the generation that suffered and got on with life, conscious that the older generations had made far greater sacrifices.

I mulled this over for a long time. I recalled my uncle telling me of the trip he had taken with his parents to the First World War battlefields of northern France. At the age of nineteen, his father, Owen, had been part of the British Expeditionary Force sent to defend Mons against the first German advance. The retreat entailed a forced march along roads to the coast clogged with refugees and casualties, and the men had marched without rest or food on bleeding feet for more than a week. Like others, Owen claimed to have seen a great angel hovering overhead as men tossed their boots and greatcoats aside and improvised pampooties from cloth strips, which they wrapped around their pulped flesh so they could tread onwards, step by painful step. A week later, before they'd had the chance to recover, the battalion was posted to defend the British position along the banks of the Aisne. On the day of his twentieth birthday, 14 September 1914, Owen had been perched behind a haycock when artillery fire struck his right arm. He was found and brought to a field hospital, where the doctors amputated his arm at the elbow.

'It is quite remarkable when you consider the chaos of the time,' Charles said, 'that, over forty years later, my father could point out the exact spot where it had happened. He said he could feel the pain still.'

There had been a pause after that. I couldn't quite remember how we had come to be having this conversation while standing on the threshold of the pantry, the trolley loaded with the night's dinner-plates stalled beside us, but Owen had died two weeks before I was born and I was eager to hear any stories about him. 'It was,' Charles continued, 'the best thing that could have happened to him, or so he used to say, for it meant he had to be assigned to desk jobs for the remainder of the war.'

Dr Khourie looked up from his notes to see if we were ready. Although the doctor had met neither of us before, he seemed able to take quick measure of his patient. With a steady gaze at Charles, he began without bluff or bonhomie: 'I think, Mr Guinness, you have sarcoidosis.' This was, he explained, a malfunction of the immune system, also known as Hutchinson's disease, which led to the build-up of sarcoids, or knots of fibrous tissue, in the lungs and throughout the body. He asked Charles whether he suffered from night sweats. My uncle nodded slowly. The granulomas on his face and hands, his watery eyes and the arthritis in his fingers were all attributable to a condition that, Dr Khourie added in a curious afterthought, was more commonly found in horses than in humans.

'Is it progressive?' I asked, when he had finished.

'No, usually the symptoms disappear by themselves, but I think in your uncle's case, the condition is chronic and has caused discomfort for quite some time. Is that so, Mr Guinness?' Once again, my uncle nodded a little sadly.

His lungs were very congested, the doctor said, and he would expect some scarring of the pulmonary lining. He would have to order a biopsy to confirm his diagnosis and to check whether Charles was suffering from any other form of lung disease disguised by the condition. However, the good news was that if it was indeed sarcoidosis, the treatment would be straightforward: a course of steroids on which he could remain for some time. The condition was incurable, but the symptoms and the further spread of sarcoids could be very effectively controlled. There was no reason to fear any reduction in his quality of life. For the moment, he would prescribe Charles some antibiotics and a cortisone inhaler, which should allow a little more air into his lungs and help with the atrocious cough.

This sounded better than either of us had expected. I noticed a wave of relief pass over Charles's face, combined with a sense of wonder that the mysteries of the body could be so easily solved of a morning. For my part, I felt chastened by the simple fact that all this time my uncle had suffered needlessly.

'Do you live with him?' Dr Khourie asked me, as the door closed behind Charles, who had gone out to the reception area.

'Yes, I do.'

'Well, you can help greatly by keeping his environment as dust-free as possible.' He recommended a brand of hypo-allergenic duvet, which I noted down with some remorse, thinking of the antique pillows, the feather eiderdown, and the grey curls of felted dust I had lifted from the books beside his bed the last time his room was spring-cleaned.

'One other thing,' the doctor said, as I replaced the pen in my bag. 'Sometimes this condition can affect the nervous system and cause depression. Once he's on steroids, his energy will return quickly and he should feel fine. But in the meantime, please call me if you notice any change in his moods.'

I thanked Dr Khourie warmly, and returned to the waiting room. Charles was sitting on a bench, his scarf pulled lopsidedly around his neck, looking a little like Paddington Bear. His eyes anxiously searched out mine for any hint of graver news. I shook my head and smiled. Tucking my right hand beneath his elbow, I guided him to his feet and we set off slowly down the stairs together, step by careful step, for with my left hand on the rail I found I had no way of wiping away the tears that blurred our uncertain descent.

'I feel like a young man of twenty again,' Charles says. It is lunch-time, and I have just finished recounting our honeymoon trek to Machu Picchu, trying to convey the full wonder of the Urubamba Valley and the caracaras that flitted from rock to rock. Two shallow saucers carved out of the mountain stone and filled with water in a roofless classroom had served as mirrors, the guide told us, to instruct the Inca children in astronomy. 'How remarkable,' Charles murmurs, accommodating this nugget among others about Inca society gleaned during our absence from William Prescott's *History of the Conquest of Peru*, which he had retrieved from the bookshelves in the study before we set off.

While we have been travelling to the farthest corners of Peru, my uncle tells me that he has found the outpatients department of Tallaght Hospital to be almost as exotic. The international cast of medics who have ushered him from one test to another fascinate him as evidence of Dublin's new-found cosmopolitanism, of which he eagerly approves. The bronchoscopy, he admits, was most unpleasant, although the sheer novelty of having to swallow a camera ('like something Q might have invented for 007') provided its own compensation. He seems rather pleased to have managed it all on his own. When I ask whether he hasn't been bored during the long hours of waiting, he shrugs and says he has found the reception areas to be quite comfortable, providing a warm place to read his book. The results have come back positive for sarcoidosis, and although the X-rays reveal extensive and irreparable scarring of his internal tissues, there are no signs of any other disease.

Charles has been transformed by cortisone. He has put on

sufficient weight to jettison the sash cord he used to belt his trousers in loose tucks around his waist. I notice that the strawberry patches on his face are beginning to fade a little in colour, and his eyes seem less red. At night, he used to stop on the return of the stair to gasp for breath before unfolding the shutters across the arched window; now I hear him continue on upstairs, the necessary task forgotten. When he does stop to look out, it is to admire the new colours in the Pleasure Grounds, as the side-garden has always been called. Our wedding guests gave us vouchers for a nearby nursery, and I've been planting out the newly cleared beds: phlox and silver-leaved forget-me-nots clumped in together; pink hardy geraniums splashed against the yellow day lilies.

There is no improvement in my uncle's arthritis. To the children's delight, he still opens his crisps each lunch-time by plucking a biro from his top pocket and stabbing the packet vigorously, cursing as the contents predictably explode over the carpet below. He is more discreet about his inhaler, turning aside to take off his glasses and peer at the label to check the canister is the right way up before squeezing it in his fist, his eyes popping as he wheezes in deeply and feels the sudden benefit of all that new space in his chest. He is slightly indignant to discover that several friends are asthmatics who have been using inhalers all this time without his ever noticing. One of them even has the temerity to have put up with sarcoidosis for years under the guise of being cursed with 'a weak chest'.

Mindful that I am to return to work in September, I negotiate with Charles to share the costs of keeping the house dust-free. I put up an ad in the local supermarket for a part-time housekeeper. Three women reply, but two return back down the drive without ringing the doorbell, having sized up the job at a glance. The third, Patricia O'Rourke, arrives wearing a strapless floral tea-dress, jacket and sunglasses, accessorized for a garden party. She replied to the ad, she tells me, because she has been a housekeeper in big houses all her life, having started out in service with Garret FitzGerald. I notice her taking in the avalanche of papers and the dusty curtains, and her slight smile of recognition at the shambles. No, she replies, in response to my query, the scale of the task doesn't faze her, as long as she can take it bit by bit and tackle a different room each week. When she goes, Charles remarks that, while she seems highly competent, he fears she 'might be a bit grand for us'.

Over the summer, a pattern of domesticity emerges. Patricia comes on Wednesday mornings, occasionally bringing with her a bag of home-made meringues. She finds my uncle 'kind of old-fashioned'; this refers chiefly to his practice of asking her to step outside the drawing room while he puts the day's wages into a brown envelope rather than handing over a wad of ready cash. Charles, once he realizes nothing else is expected of him, accepts the new arrangement without a murmur.

Patricia's curiosity about the house sets me thinking about Muriel. The last time I visited her was in late November, when Charles and I drove down to see her and her sister, Ethel, at Rathcabban.

Muriel had made scones for tea. She was on a walking frame, but she still looked the sturdier of the two sisters as she moved about the table. Their small house was warm and comfortable. Charles seemed at ease, filling Muriel in on parish news and recounting what local gossip he had picked up from Susie.

On the way there he had told me a story about the Countess of Rosse, who was apparently considered too *beau monde* for Birr. An early patron of the fashion designer Norman Hartnell, she had gone to visit one of her tenants in what Charles described as a 'squalid, damp, poky little cottage'. The tenant had seized the opportunity to outline all its deficiencies, the draughty windows, the leaking roof, the poor plumbing, and was mid-way through her tale when the Countess threw up her hands in horror and proclaimed, 'But, my dear, you mustn't change a thing. It's all So You!'

He had chuckled gleefully at this, but the anecdote prompted me to consider whether my own behaviour hadn't been similarly crass at times. When I was seventeen and in my final year at school, I had been invited to the Trinity Ball by a friend. As the ball was on a Friday, and there was school the next day at St Columba's, my father had told me that I would need Charles's permission to go. Mindful of the school's restrictions on day pupils, my uncle said no.

At seventeen, this edict seemed so obvious an injustice it could plainly be disregarded. On the night of the ball, I dutifully said goodnight, went up to bed and waited. The plan was to catch the last 47B into town, where Brian would pick me up outside the Metropole. I could take a taxi home at dawn in sufficient time to answer Charles's wake-up call. What could go wrong? I packed my dress and some jeans into a bag and stuffed my bed with pillows. When I heard Charles enter the bathroom, I crept downstairs to the back door, still dressed in my pyjamas in case I was discovered, and opened the shutters, creak by echoing creak, to let myself out. Once clear of the house, I changed into my jeans and top, stashed my pyjamas in the bushes and hurried on down the drive with half an hour to spare. It was only when I reached the corner of Tibradden Road that I thought to look for my bus fare. I rooted through my pockets, and then through my bag as it began to dawn on me that, while I had four shades of eye-shadow, I had forgotten to pack my purse. There was nothing for it but to return and pick it up; if I hurried I could still make it back for the last bus.

I ran up the drive and went straight round to the back of the house. A short flight of steps led to the back door, and from the bottom of these I could see with horror that someone had closed the shutters in the minutes I'd been gone. I turned the key and pushed the door open gently. It was no use: the shutters were barred across. My two options now were to ring the front-door bell and brave the reaction of my uncle and grandmother with unimaginable consequences, or to go down to the kitchen and see whether I could convince Muriel to let me fetch the purse from my bedroom without raising the alarm.

Through the basement window I could see Muriel sitting at the table, a steaming mug cupped between her two hands. She was staring into the middle distance while the radio rattled on. I flushed with shame, for what I would ask of her, and for the alarm my knocking was about to cause. Eight years earlier, an IRA raid on the house had begun in just the same way, with a banging at the kitchen door. On that occasion it had been Joe Kirwan who banged on the glass, calling out that Joseph had been taken ill at the lodge; he needed to call an ambulance. Muriel had thought his grimaces looked odd through the window, but, putting them down to reasonable distress, she opened the door to let him in. A man who had been hiding against the wall, his gun in Joe's side, jumped out immediately. Two others then followed him inside. They locked up my grandmother, Muriel and Kathleen with Joe in the coal cellar while they took Charles at gunpoint around the house, to show them where the silver and shotguns were stored.

'Who's there?' Muriel called out now, standing back from the door and squinting hard through the window.

'It's me,' I said, pressing my face to the glass. 'I'm locked out. I'll explain it all if you let me in. It's all right, I'm on my own.'

Slowly she drew back the bolts and stood aside to let me pass into the kitchen, a look of grave suspicion on her face. I sat down on the chair she pointed to and, avoiding her gaze, outlined my plan as best I could. The things that could go wrong seemed to have suddenly multiplied and my plea to be allowed upstairs to collect my purse resounded hollowly in this setting. It would not be fair to let Brian down, I reasoned. No one need be any the wiser.

That statement hung in the air. All she said by way of reproof, her lips pursed, was: 'And your grandmother is sick in bed.'

True, the doctor had visited my grandmother earlier in the week and had advised her to rest as much as she could. But it was just another of her periodic turns, she said; next week, she would be up and about as usual, resuming the writing of her memoirs and the running of the household.

'She won't ever know,' I said.

'What if she got up in the night and came to check on you and found you weren't there?' asked Muriel, quietly. 'It would kill her.'

I had no answer. It seemed to me unlikely that my grand-mother ever came into my bedroom while I was asleep, but perhaps Muriel knew better. An expression of profound disap-pointment had settled around her mouth and I found my arguments collapsing under the sudden realization of how much her good opinion of me mattered. There was a long silence. It was past eleven o'clock. Even if I ran, I would scarcely catch the bus now. 'Can I make you some cocoa?' she asked presently, and I noticed the absence of my name in the offer. I nodded, acknowledging defeat.

She went out to the scullery then to take a scoop of milk from the big basin. 'Muriel,' I asked, raising my unsteady voice, 'can I just try and call the Metropole first and see whether someone in the ticket office might go out and tell him I'm not coming?'

'Go on ahead, Selina,' came the reply. But at the other end of the line, the cinema phone just rang and rang.

I remained vigilant over the coming days for any clues that my uncle and grandmother had been told of my exploits, but there were none. I concluded that Muriel had kept our encounter to herself, and she never once alluded to the events of that night, but I noticed her registering my new depth of regard.

6.

We are in Athlone, where we have been spending New Year with friends, when Colin receives a rare call from Charles on his mobile. His voice is feeble and hesitant. 'I was wondering when you might be planning to come home? The thing is I can't quite manage to get downstairs to feed the cat this morning. It was a bit of an ordeal yesterday.'

Three days ago, we left him cheerfully reading through the scenario sent by a cousin for a murder mystery party she was hosting on New Year's Eve. Charles had been allocated the role of 'a rather louche, Chekhovian doctor' for which he had retrieved a smoking jacket and stethoscope from the depths of the dressing-up cupboard where the odds and ends of past pantomimes were stored. As we were leaving, he muttered that he hoped to be among the first victims on the night so that he could turn in early, but I smiled at this, thinking that once he got there he would begin to enjoy himself.

We say goodbye to our friends and leave immediately. The drive back to Dublin gives me the chance to reflect on the holidays. Thinking about it, I realize that my uncle removed himself a little from this year's festivities, that there have been small signs that all was not well. On Christmas Day he attended Holy Communion rather than come with us to the family service, and most evenings, when better fare was on offer in the kitchen below, he chose to eat alone in the dining room.

79

Through the autumn he had been in almost rude health, continuing to fatten to his own satisfaction and to gain control over the cough that seemed to trouble him a little less at night. Whether the diagnosis had lifted the burden of fear, or whether it was just that our initial visit had broken his habit of self-neglect, he no longer dodged the doctor, instead keeping the hospital appointments he faithfully scribbled down in his pocket diary. A new ease entered our conversations. The vanities and minor politics of academia amused him, schooled as he was in the way that staff rooms magnify the idiosyncrasies of colleagues. He listened and offered parallels, taken not from his own life but from literature, such as Anthony Trollope's *Can You Forgive Her?*, or his favourite book, Voltaire's *Candide*.

We arrive home in the afternoon to find Charles sitting huddled by the unlit fire in the drawing room, an old cricket sweater pulled over his pyjama top and a shawl slipping off his shoulders. He manages a faint smile but makes no attempt to stand. His breathing is shallow and rapid, and I am alarmed to find his skin clammy. On the sofa are his old eiderdown and pillow, with the familiar jar of Vicks VapoRub lying lidless on the carpet. I ask him if he slept here last night and he nods, and gasps out that he couldn't manage the stairs. He is far worse than his call led us to believe.

I settle him as comfortably as I can, while Colin goes to dismantle Charles's bed and bring it downstairs. When we called Dr Khourie's practice from Athlone, we were transferred to a locum, whose car arrives as I am making up the bed. He bustles in and, after a brisk but careful examination, diagnoses bronchitis. The sarcoidosis, he warns, increases the risk that this might develop into a full-blown pulmonary infection and for this reason he would usually advise hospital admission. However, the locum continues while writing out a prescription, we might be better off treating him at home, given the virulent outbreak of the winter vomiting bug across the city's hospitals. We are to keep him warm and hydrated, and take him to A&E at the first sign of any deterioration.

Colin shows the doctor out and goes to fetch the prescription from the chemist. When I return to the drawing room, Charles is clearly weighing up the doctor's words in his own mind. 'Would you prefer us to take you down to the Adelaide straight away?' I ask gently. He pulls a face and shrugs. He looks too tired to make a decision either way. We agree that I will call the surgery again in the morning, and wait to see whether the antibiotics grant him any overnight improvement, aided by a little soup and some rest.

When I look in on him later, he is awake and his breathing seems a little less laboured, although his cough has returned with all its old force.

'Did you ever get to the party, Uncle?' I ask.

'Yes,' he replies. 'Felt ill at dinner, though . . .' he pauses to raise himself up on his pillow '. . . but I didn't want to let the host down.' He falls silent, so I sit down next to him on the floor.

'Were you murdered quickly?' I ask, hoping to cheer him up a little.

'Mercifully, yes. By a nice woman too, not who I thought it would be.'

It is clear, after a while, that the lulls in our conversation are due to more than lack of breath. He has something on his mind. I wait it out. Eventually he announces he has a confession to make.

'I took your car.' He watches narrowly for my reaction, a glint of amusement in his eyes.

'What do you mean, you took my car?'

'My car wouldn't start, so I drove yours,' he says, as evenly as he can.

'But how did you manage without the radiator?' My Opel Astra has been off the road for a month. The air-conditioning is broken, so when it rains the windscreen fogs up instantly.

'I drove,' he says, and then he stops, for a rising chuckle has triggered a fit of coughing. He waits till he has fully regained his breath, then continues, 'I drove with the window open. And you know,' his palm mimes a circle, 'I wiped the windscreen from time to time.'

'But it was raining, wasn't it? At least it was in Athlone.'

'Just a little,' says Charles, an abashed smile brightening his face. 'But there was no one on the roads. It was quite all right.' For a man who lovingly regards his AA membership sticker as a proficiency badge in motoring, this hazard seems entirely out of character.

He drops his hand to give mine a squeeze. 'Don't be cross with me, darling.'

I find it hard to hold his gaze. A log shifts in the grate. He looks feverish and, suddenly, very old.

'Of course I'm not cross,' I whisper. 'You're forgiven. Don't worry any more about it.' I stand to kiss him on the forehead and say goodnight.

Down in the kitchen, I vigorously wash up his bowl. Despite what I said, I am cross, very cross. 'Stupid man,' I mutter to myself, 'stupid, stupid man,' thinking not of the car, but of his lungs. And yet, later, when I'm getting ready for bed, I recall the note of triumph in his voice. 'Stupid man,' I say out loud. But this time I find myself pronouncing the words with a consoling sense of wonder and respect. With that spirit, surely he will pull through.

*

On 6 January, my departmental administrator calls me out of a lunchtime class. Charles has been taken by ambulance to the A&E department in Tallaght with suspected pneumonia. I make arrangements to leave immediately.

I find Colin and Charles in a cubicle. My uncle is sitting on the trolley in his dressing-gown, breathing through an oxygen mask, a tall cylinder beside him. He raises his hand in the barest of greetings. Colin signals me outside. He tells me they have been waiting to see the registrar since ten o'clock so that he can be assessed for a bed on one of the respiratory wards. 'He says he feels like he is drowning. All I can do is hold his hand.' My father and stepmother are on their way to the hospital.

Charles lies on the trolley and keeps his eyes closed, biding his time between fits of coughing. He is too weak to talk. Colin helps him use a bedpan. Throughout the afternoon, nurses come in and out to collect syringes and swabs from the cupboards behind us, for it turns out this extra space is properly a storage area that has been curtained off to afford some privacy. Out in the corridor, there are more elderly patients sitting in armchairs. The clutter of IV stands and the various sports bags and yellow bin-liners of belongings do not leave much of a passageway between the armchairs, lined up against one wall, and the trolleys opposite. While queuing for the bathroom, I topple against one woman sitting in her dressing-gown on the edge of her trolley. When I apologize, she tells me it's her third day out here in the corridor. She has been admitted with chest pains and is awaiting tests. Her son lounges across the bottom of her trolley, texting busily. The doors to the reception area bang open suddenly and three paramedics rush past us, kicking belongings aside and shouting, 'Clear the way, coming through.' I glimpse a girl on the trolley, her head in a brace, a tube in her mouth, her eyes fearfully open, before they bang through the second doors into a theatre at the end of the passage and disappear. 'Car crash, poor love,' says the woman, not quite resigned to it yet. 'God, it's mayhem out there.'

After dinner, all visitors are ushered out. Charles is not going to get a bed tonight. Instead his trolley is wheeled out of the examination area and placed next to the nurses' station. 'Like the army,' Charles gasps, when he sees me looking upset. 'Bunks on trains. Sleep anywhere.'

'I'll keep an eye on him,' a nurse promises, watching me fuss over him, reluctant to leave. 'Go on now, away with you.'

Charles spends the next two days in A&E. Then, on Thursday morning, just as one of the anaesthetists is passing on his rounds, he howls out loud. 'I'll sort this out,' the anaesthetist says, and rushes away. We overhear a strident discussion on the telephone. Ten minutes later, Charles is admitted to Intensive Care.

When we are allowed in to visit some time later, he has a tube in his mouth connecting him to a respirator. Behind his left shoulder, a machine wheezes steadily as it pushes air into his lungs. The ICU registrar explains the rest. He will not know until he receives the lab results whether the pneumonia is bacterial or caused by a virus. In the meantime they are administering three different antibiotics intravenously and they have begun to drain the large amount of fluid from his pulmonary cavity. He is on pain relief. If I want to provide him some comfort, I am allowed to moisten little pink sponges on sticks, like lollipops, and swab them around his lips and mouth; he is not allowed to swallow because the water will go straight to his lungs.

The bright white light overhead, the full rig of equipment banked behind the bed, with its sundry leads and LED displays, the curtains that hang down either side: it is unnervingly clinical and public. It is as if my uncle has been set up on a stage and, like any audience, we have been asked to keep our distance and wait. He wears white anti-embolism stockings to his knees, his toes exposed grotesquely to the air. The nurse has soaked a blue cloth in water and placed it on his forehead to keep him cool. With his eyes closed, my uncle is dwarfed by these machines that seem to live here parasitically on his frail body; but of course, I remind myself, it is the other way round.

On his second day in ICU, Charles gestures to my father for a pencil and paper. He scrawls notes for Colin to bring home. We are taking it in turns to visit each morning and evening.

The note says: 'Throat sore because of tube. Can't be helped. There have been lots of doctors. All reassuring. The beds are nice and separate so one feels private. One also has one nurse each. A nurse shaved me last night – lovely relief! I'd love you to stay but I may doze.' It ends: 'You can show Selina my epistles.'

On the evening of the tenth, encouraged by his progress, the doctors remove him from the respirator. When I arrive the next morning I am surprised to find the tube back in place. The registrar explains quietly, 'He went into failure.' I stand there for a minute, stunned, unsure what degree of departure these words convey.

'Hello, Uncle,' I whisper. He smiles a greeting with his eyes, but it is brief. I can see his spirits are low. I put my hand over his and am pleased when a few minutes later his eyes close and he appears to fall asleep. Today's nurse, Michael, suggests that after the weekend, the doctors will perform a tracheotomy. This is a small incision made below his vocal cords so the respirator tube can be attached through his windpipe. It will, he says, be more comfortable for Charles and allow him to whisper. 'More permanent, too?' I ask.

'No, I shouldn't think so,' he says. 'He should breathe independently once the infection is beaten. It will leave a small scar; that's all.'

When he wakes up, Charles gestures for the letter board that Michael has provided. His index finger wavers over each letter, making the job of piecing the message together quite difficult. He gets frustrated with me quickly and shakes his head with frank impatience at how slow I am. Eventually, I make out the words 'Last night horrid', the last word spelled out twice for emphasis. 'Conversation with yr father yesterday, great weight off my mind,' comes next, followed by 'Affairs in order.' He finishes, and lets me set the board down. Thinking our conversation might be exerting him too much, I ask whether he wants me to leave for a little while, and his hand shoots out like a claw to grasp my own. Picking up the board a second time, he indicates that the clergyman who visited him earlier had to be encouraged (this word underlined in the air) to say a prayer. He opens and shuts his eyes to pantomime his amazement.

The next day I arrive to find Charles asleep, so I sit and mark my students' essays on *King Lear*. When his eyes open, he barely registers my presence. He looks anguished and far away, his spirits receding to some place of great turmoil. I whisper reassurances to him but he doesn't turn his head to face me for some time. 'What is it?' I repeat, till he reaches for the letter board and with great effort spells out, 'When I die, where shall I go?'

'Where you expect,' I answer, after a moment. 'Where you have always believed you will go.'

He shakes his head vehemently and tries again: 'Where shall

my body go?' He has tears in his eyes. 'Shall I stay here?' he insists, his finger hitting the board with frustration at each letter.

I struggle hard towards an answer. 'No,' I begin. 'You won't stay here.' He is crying now, and I have seen him cry only once before, at his mother's funeral.

I am stalling. What I think he wants to know is how his body will get home should he die here, and I do not want to hear myself explain what will happen. In all the time we have been together, Charles and I have talked with great lightness of things, particularly when they have been most deeply felt. In all the years he has cared for me, my uncle has never made any demands on me, except to believe always in my honesty; even when he shouldn't have.

'No, we will take you home,' I tell him, as steadily as I can. 'Back to Tibradden, and when the time comes we will take you down to Whitechurch, to Horace, and we will bury you with your mother and father as you have always planned. You will be committed to their keeping and God's.'

He is listening with his eyes fixed on a point above me and I still cannot tell whether I have understood him right. I want to add to this that he is far from dying, that he will fight on longer, but how, when I see him this exhausted, can I impose such a wish? So quietly I wipe my own face, and reach to wipe his, and only then his eyes turn towards me, and I realize that what I have said opens no abyss, for his faith is greater and far exceeds any consolation I can provide. To care is enough.

On my way out, I notice the empty chapel. I have passed it every day but have never felt like entering it till now. I find a Bible in a pew, and hunt for the tale of how Martha, the sister too busy with her chores to listen to Christ, fetched Him to raise her brother Lazarus from the tomb. 'Our friend Lazarus has fallen asleep, but I am going there to awaken him.' When I lean forward and attempt to pray, it feels as though someone has applied a damper to the echo of machines. I yearn into the dark, trying too hard to listen.

'And how is poor Master Charles?' demands Susie, as she grips the roof of the car to lever herself out one Friday morning in early February.

'A bit better, Susie,' I reply cheerfully. This has become a stock response. In truth, the best the nurses can say is that the antibiotics are holding the infection in check while they gradually reduce the levels of respiratory assistance. The tracheotomy allows Charles to speak in a whisper, and since he was moved to an isolation room within the Intensive Care Unit he has found it easier to sleep. His spirits have improved and he is stronger now. Sometimes when I visit, he chooses to pick up the pencil and paper he has at his bed-side so he can write private communiqués telling me what he has learned from his conversations with the staff. Indicating the nurse at the end of his bed, the last note read: 'His father runs the Jordanian Army so you must pay him great respect.'

It has taken me a while to realize that the unit discourages its nurses from offering the prognoses that we relatives desperately seek. Plans for the future are actively discouraged, for the only tense in Intensive Care is the treatable present. 'Wait till we get him onto a ward' is the formula, implying that once he is there time will extend and allow for everything.

Every Friday when she comes for her wages, Susie asks when Master Charles can be expected home. Her insistent enquiries are prompted by more than fondness: Charles's illness has revealed the uncertainty of her family's own situation. She is sharply attuned to the dying note and I find it hard to cope with her anxiety on top of my own. I pay their wages on behalf of Charles but know no more than they what the future holds for Tibradden.

'What news is there of Master Niall?' she asks, almost idly, as if this were just polite conversation; but she has posed the same question to me every Friday for the past six weeks. Her interest in my brother's life has intensified markedly since Charles was admitted to hospital. My answers have not varied much. Niall and I are in touch, but not frequently enough to satisfy Susie's thirst for news. Again I tell her that he is getting on well in the south of Spain, and explain once more as best I can what he does for a living, which is something far removed from my world and light years away from Susie's. Niall is a football analyst. This means he spends his day watching games played in the German second division via satellite, before emailing his match assessments to a professional gambler in London. The gambler then bets on the strength of Niall's recommendations, and Niall gets paid according to his winnings. 'It's a bit like being a stockbroker,' he told me once, and this I relay to Susie, who nods sagely.

'Hasn't he turned into a fine gentleman!' she exclaims. Her eyes shine as she moves swiftly on to the matter she really cares about: 'Do you think, Miss Selina, that he'll ever settle back here?'

'Possibly,' I say, 'but he does seem very happy in Spain.'

'And sure why wouldn't he, with the fine weather over there?' She inspects her fingernails for a few moments. 'All the same, he would miss Tibradden.'

There is a leading pause.

'Indeed,' I reply. 'Though, if you think about it, Susie, he has never actually lived here.'

A stack of post from the Department of Agriculture sits on the table in front of me. Charles has given me no instructions about running the farm in his absence, bar advising that Joe gets paid extra for bank holidays. This morning I spent an hour opening envelopes to discover that agricultural bureaucracy has an arcane language all its own. There are notices about changes in headage payments, and EU stocking directives, and new regulations for the spreading of nitrates, and some forms marked 'urgent', which I have no idea how to fill in. One circular tells me how to obtain passports for cattle; another asks my uncle to please return his sheep census, which is now overdue. Both concepts strike me as absurd, but I'm hoping Susie will put me right.

'Sixty-eight,' she says, pointing her shaky finger at the first box on the census. 'That would be sixty-eight ewes that Master Charles would have.'

I write in '68' next to 'total size of flock', and am about to move on to the next question when Susie fixes me with a sudden stare.

'Would you count the hoggets in that number?' she asks, and takes the paper from me to peer more closely. I haven't seen her wear glasses in years.

'I don't know, Susie. What's a hogget?'

She smiles. I perceive her satisfaction at gaining the upper hand.

'Sure, Miss Selina, it's a ewe that hasn't yeaned. A year old, a female.' She pronounces ewe as 'yo'. I scan through the pages and, to my relief, find a separate box marked 'hogget'.

'Let me see now,' says Susie, nursing a frown as she closes her eyes to concentrate. 'I think there'd be twenty-four, or is it twenty-three, over on the Ladies' Meadows? Wait a minute and I'll ask Joe.'

Waving aside my protest that the missing figure can be filled in at the end, she pushes herself up and shuffles out to the hall. 'Joe!' she roars. I join her on the front steps as Joe comes bolting around the side of the house.

'Yes, Susie,' he calls, his voice impatient. Seeing me, his tone moderates: 'I was just seeing how you were off for wood.'

Susie sighs. 'Never mind that now. Miss Selina here wants to know how many hoggets are beyond in the Ladies' Meadows.'

He scratches his head and looks nervous. 'Let me see . . .'

'It's just for the Department of Agriculture, a form for their statistics,' I explain. 'I'm sure a rough estimate will do.'

'Oh, no, Miss Selina, you have to get these things right,' Susie insists. 'You'd never know when these people would be trying to catch you out.'

'Twenty-four,' Joe says, with sudden certainty.

'There you are, Miss Selina, twenty-four.' Without a word to her husband, Susie shuffles into the house, leaving me to thank him and follow after.

Their son, Joseph, is in the back of the car, twiddling his habitual length of baler twine, his dark head bent in concentration on the task. He doesn't look up as I approach and pause by the window to greet him.

'How's he doing?' I ask Joe.

'Grand,' he replies, trying to muster a smile. He has one foot in the driver's door, and he turns to say something to Joseph as he gets in. I peer through the window and wave.

'Fuck off,' says Joseph. His voice is a loud and perfect replica of his mother's, though I can't imagine her thinking 'Fuck off' let alone saying it. 'Would you ever fuck off yourself!' I'm impressed. They are the clearest words I've ever heard him pronounce.

'Joseph, stop that,' shouts his father. Joseph gives a high cackle in response and starts to rock backwards and forwards, laughing gleefully.

I assure Joe he is not to mind, I've heard worse, but he doesn't reply. At the door of the house, I turn to say goodbye and see him staring straight down the drive, the figure of his son swaying in the back seat.

On Valentine's Day, I bring Charles a bunch of snowdrops from the garden. He has finally been weaned off the respirator and onto a machine called a 'BiPAP', which, the nurse explains, will give each breath he draws a bit of extra pressure to fill out his lungs. Today is the first day he has been permitted to eat solids and I find him polishing off a tub of raspberry yoghurt. 'I don't think I have ever tasted anything so good,' he declares, giving the plastic spoon one last lick before turning his attention to me and asking for news.

I tell him that for the past couple of days I have been pruning the apple trees in the old walled garden, and have cleared the top quarter where the strawberries used to be so that we can start growing our own vegetables. 'Well, don't exhaust yourself,' he says. But it isn't a chore. I've been trying to return to writing my thesis, without success. Rather than sit at my desk and stare idly at the lime tree before succumbing to insomnia, it seems better to seek the bracing virtues of fresh air, dirt and birdsong and find something easier to cultivate than academic prose.

The briars have taken over in the walled garden since the gardener, Paddy Flanagan, retired fifteen years ago. In his day, neat paths of river gravel used to divide the half-acre into four, with each quarter arranged differently to accommodate nursery beds and cold-frames tucked under the sheltering hedges. When we arrived, I could not get beyond the first ten feet inside the green wooden door and so it has remained, always too great a task to begin in the time available. But the past few weeks I have found it easier than expected to cut away the undergrowth along the main path, a few metres at a time. Mats of leonine aconites, yellow and frilled, have somehow survived beneath the tall bracken, and budding clumps of blue wood anemones are interspersed through the box hedges that have grown into leggy trees. A thicket of moss roses stands where the paths used to intersect. Their rotting hips speckle the sphagnum below, beads on a viridian pillow. Crouching among the roots, I imagine myself an insect in a pre-Raphaelite window stumbling upon a fairy tale, wrapped in the smell of the earth.

Stem by thorny stem, I have cut the moss roses back to provide space for the ladder I've propped against the trunk of the first apple tree in the old espaliered row. The training wires have rusted through and all the growth has been in the highest branches beyond the reach of my shears. Unsure whether it will help or hinder, I have pruned the lower boughs, bearded with verdigris lichen, back to their first buds. When I finish, the trees resemble windblown hawthorns, the top whips still tangled together in their scramble towards the light. Standing back, they seem too slight and flimsy to bear any fruit at all.

At long last, Charles has been moved out of ICU and onto a ward. He rises to greet me when I enter. 'I stood for five minutes yesterday, on my own!' he tells me proudly. In the next bed, his neighbour repeats this news to his pillow. 'He talks to his dead wife, poor chap,' my uncle confides in a whisper. 'I had to call the nurses at about two in the morning last night because he was so upset when she answered back. He doesn't usually give her a chance to get a word in edgeways.'

It is the end of February, and Charles has been here over two weeks with an oxygen cylinder beside his bed for whenever he feels he needs it. He no longer requires the BiPAP or the catheter, and is able to feed himself. The doctors have told me that if he continues to recover his strength, they will be able to discharge him soon. The occupational therapist promises to make a home visit to assess how Charles's physical environment might be best adapted to meet his needs and gives me a list of the grants available. She explains that usually very minimal levels of intervention are required. I nod, trying not to look doubtful as I privately figure out how to square her suggestions for hand-rails and stair lifts with the council's inclusion of the house on the list of protected structures. In the meantime she promises to find me a dental technician who might make a new plate, for somehow Charles's dentures were lost in the transfer to the ward. Having so recently regained the ability to swallow, he complains, it seems a cruel fate to lose the ability to chew.

Visitors come and go throughout the week, bearing crosswords and detective novels and the gentle gossip he is eager to share. I bring him the new translation of Joseph Roth's novel *The Radetzky March*. He sucks in his lips when I give it to him and, unusually, fails to thank me. I wonder what I have done wrong as he turns the paperback over in his hands, seeming to weigh it up in his mind. 'I have always wanted to read Roth,' he eventually admits, 'but I promised myself I would wait until I had the time to read this one in the original German.' A television perched on the wall facing us is running the current episode of *Coronation Street*. 'I'll see whether I have the concentration for it,' he says, passing it back to me. I add it, a little sadly, to the pile on his bedside locker. I had hoped this saga of the Hapsburg Empire would prove an escape from the noise of the ward. I had wondered, too, whether he would recognize himself in the District Commissioner: the quiet heir to principles of service that long outlived the power and wealth of those who had established them.

Any talk about the future of the farm can be postponed until Charles is discharged. It would seem unkind in any case to encroach upon his territory of the mind with the reminder that real maps describe it, that the grass still grows. But Joe and Susie are anxious to visit. When I tentatively broach this possibility, he bites his lip and turns to the window, looking distressed. He would be afraid, he says after a moment, of upsetting Susie, and what with Joseph to mind, arranging a visit could be awkward for them. He would prefer to see them when he gets home. I understand. The seagulls are flying up over the hospital car park, blown about in the gusts of spring. 'I don't really know what to do,' he quietly admits, as we watch them glide and wheel around each other. 'They are both getting so old; Joe must be in his mid-seventies. The land would be better leased out entirely. But what would happen to them, then?' He voices this last question softly, while still watching the birds, without wanting or anticipating an answer.

Back home, I stand at the bedroom window and look out at the Lawn. The ground is thick with hummocks of last year's grass. Twenty or so sheep graze lightly over it. One or two move forward on their knees. If the land were leased out, Joe and Susie could finally retire. I know Charles has paid the stamps entitling them to a state pension. It would be perfectly practical for them to continue living in the gate-lodge while another farmer took over grazing the fields on an annual agreement. As it is, the fields beyond the Ladies' Meadows have been let for many years to tillage contractors. But, as Charles implied, it is not these practical considerations that present the impasse. Farming Tibradden is the rhythm and the routine, the prayer and the pattern, of the Kirwans' lives. Without it, Susie would regard herself as cast out, bereft. Joe is feeling his age more, I think. Some mornings, I've noticed him prolong our conversation to gain a little ease before he gets on with the lonely day ahead. If the Kirwans admit an end to their working lives, it will also bring forward the question of how long they are capable of caring for Joseph.

*

Through March, Charles regains sufficient strength to take short walks along the corridor. Then I arrive one day in April and find that, without warning, his ward has been quarantined due to the outbreak of a hospital super-bug, MRSA. The nurse on duty allows him to stand at one end of the corridor while I wait at the other. He is wearing a red paisley dressing-gown and a nasal tube that has been disconnected from its tank of oxygen so he can greet me. We wave at each other. It is the closest we will get for ten days.

On 21 April, just after supper, I pick up a message from the hospital on the answering machine. Charles has caught an infection called *Clostridium difficile* or *C. diff.* and has been moved to an isolation room. He is back on the BiPAP and has been given an injection of something to alleviate his anxiety. If I can visit the next morning, the consultant would like to see me.

The nurse finds an empty room for me to meet Charles's medical team. The consultant bustles in, another doctor with him, and begins abruptly. My uncle's blood gases deteriorated sharply at six o'clock this morning and, though he has settled down comfortably since, he would like me to discuss with Charles the possibility of signing a non-resuscitation order. He explains that the effect of this would be that if my uncle stopped breathing the team would be ordered not to intubate him for artificial respiration. The consultant contains himself from fidgeting while I try to think, which I find hard to do. 'But he was coming home when I last saw him' is all I want to say. I start to ask questions about the hospital bug he has caught and school myself to listen as the second doctor explains: because of the widespread damage to his lungs, if my uncle were to be intubated a second time, they think it highly unlikely that he would wean successfully from the respirator. The non-resuscitation order would be 'just a precaution,' the consultant adds, 'just so we know what his wishes are.' I ask the nurse to come with me when I go to see Charles. There is no good way to raise this, she counsels kindly, after the doctors have left the room.

Charles is breathing through a mask again. The oxygen gurgles up in bubbles from the tank each time he draws breath. Nevertheless he greets me warmly. He holds up his arms and mimes out the final irony that having been granted at last the luxury of a private bathroom he is unable to use it because of all his drips and machines. Then he notes my expression, and the presence of the nurse. The time has come for me to reassure him that he will be all right and that in a short time I will be taking him home. But this is not the message I have come to deliver. So I sit down next to him and try not to falter in my explanation of what his consultant has asked me to discuss with him. I have to put my ear against the mask to hear his low replies. He asks me how bad his lungs are, and I say, 'Not great,' rather than 'like flitters at a window', which is how I have imagined them from the consultant's description. And then we both cry. Slowly we begin to draft the impossible letter, asking that he be intubated only *in extremis*, and kept on the respirator only so long as progress is observed. The nurse reads it through for him and he agrees it expresses his wishes. When she leaves us, we sit together for a long time.

In the afternoon I drive down to Limerick, where I have to give an evening seminar. Charles will not hear of my cancelling it, telling me it will take his mind off things to hear how it has gone when I come back. Passing through the north Tipperary countryside, my attention is caught by strips of unnatural colour on the horizon. At first glance I think they are sheets of plastic laid out on the ground to protect some summer crop from late frosts. But as I draw nearer, I realize that someone is growing tulips in the Irish drizzle, acres of orange and yellow and red, with one row of blackish purple. I drive on, trying to keep this astonishing sight in my mind's eye to sustain me through the journey ahead.

I return the following evening to find that Charles has been readmitted to ICU. His nurse reassures me that his blood gases and oxygen levels have steadily improved over the course of the day. He is asleep when I enter his room, the same one he left six weeks ago, and I sit and wait for a long time, deeply grateful for the peace he enjoys. 'The nurses tell me you are not to talk,' I instruct, when he wakes up, prompting a smile at my bossiness. I tell him of the trip, of the friends I met, and of the unexpected tulips I sighted on the journey down. When I have finished my account, I tell him softly that he should rest now and imagine the colours in the field. He pulls his hand from mine and puts his finger over the valve to quiet the mask's gurgle. I put my ear to the plastic to listen. Very slowly, and very clearly, he enunciates, 'Is that what I am supposed to do?'

'Yes,' I reply, 'you are to go to sleep. Give your lungs the rest they need to continue working.' He smiles again, and presses my hand very tightly up to his face. I tell him I love him very much. He nods as his eyes close, and I wait for several minutes before I bend down to kiss him goodbye.

I am outside weeding the following afternoon when Colin takes the call. He sits down next to me on the steps to the sunken garden, and holds me as I try to gather my resolve. Outside ICU, Horace and my father are waiting, my father's arms spread wide at the sight of me to offer consolation. He hugs me very closely and tells me Charles died about half an hour ago on the operating table as they were trying to intubate him. The registrar tells us he was under anaesthetic and so didn't feel any pain.

Charles's body returns to Tibradden two days later, on our

first wedding anniversary. We lay him out in the drawing room overnight before he travels the short familiar mile down to Whitechurch. Joe and Susie come to pay their respects. They are in their best clothes. Susie's grief, so quiet a lament from so determined a woman, squeezes all the air from me. He is the sixth of the Guinnesses she has seen buried from Tibradden, the third of her employers.

The next morning is bright and cold. The family huddles on the steps while the undertakers shoulder his coffin out of the house and into the hearse. This time it is Colin who reads the Sermon on the Mount. Outside in the graveyard, the sun shines strongly and all the birds are singing. A distant cousin will comment later on how inappropriate my smile in the graveyard appeared. But as the prayers are said above the grave of his parents, I cannot stop smiling because the day is as Charles would wish it, breezy and clear, a good day for driving out somewhere on a whim to escape the rack of the world.

It is two months before I can face going through the two yellow bags of his belongings from the hospital. I pull out *The Radetzky March* and find a postcard from a friend, marking his place in chapter eight.

In the years before the Great War, at the time the events chronicled in these pages took place, it was not yet a matter of indifference whether a man lived or died. When someone was expunged from the lists of the living, someone else did not immediately step up to take his place, but a gap was left to show where he had been, and those who knew the man who had died or disappeared well or even less well, fell silent whenever they saw the gap. When a fire happened to consume a particular dwelling in a row of dwellings, the site of the conflagration remained for a long time afterwards. For masons and bricklayers worked slowly and thoughtfully, and when they walked past the ruins, neighbours and passers-by alike recalled the form and the walls of the house that had once stood there. That's how it was then! Everything that grew took long to grow; and everything that ended took a long time to be forgotten. Everything that existed left behind traces of itself, and people then lived by their memories, just as we nowadays live by our capacity to forget, quickly and comprehensively.

7.

Charles's accountant works in a fancy glass office block just off St Stephen's Green. The receptionist ushers me into one of the conference rooms on the top floor and disappears to fetch coffee. Through the bank of windows I can see out over the terraces of Long Lane and Heytesbury Street to the Dublin Mountains beyond. I try to make out which of the hills is Tibradden. It is always difficult to pick out its small dome sliding off the shoulder of Three Rock Mountain towards Glendhu.

It turns out that, several years ago, Charles set up a discretionary trust to administer his estate. His accountant, Roger, and another member of his solicitors' practice, Paul, are joint trustees. Who eventually will own Tibradden, and how Charles's assets are to be assigned, is up to them to decide. A codicil, drafted in hospital with my father's assistance, grants me a life interest in the estate until probate is cleared. This means that Colin and I can continue to live at Tibradden while Charles's affairs are being administered by the trustees. Their first task will be to obtain a complete valuation of the house, contents and land. How long the whole process will take, Roger cannot say. The Revenue will need time to reach a determination on the taxes owed, and this could take a year or more; sometimes it takes two or three. He warns me gently that most clients find the delay frustrating. In the meantime, Paul says, it would greatly help if I could hunt down some missing share certificates and financial documents, which he thinks Charles held. And if I could act as caretaker of the property, particularly in the management of the farm during this limbo period before probate is cleared, it would be of great assistance. Given that Colin and I do not own Tibradden, nor should we expect to, Paul advises us not to undertake any significant repairs to the house or major work on the land. I should just keep things ticking over as best I can.

At home there are more than a hundred exam scripts waiting to be marked. 'Have you ever visited Tibradden?' I ask the solicitor. No, never, he admits. His colleague handled Charles's affairs during his lifetime. 'There is no filing cabinet, you realize. I'll be hunting through wardrobes, and old suitcases, and rooms that haven't been cleared out for generations. It will take time.'

He smiles thinly, a little disconcerted. 'I'm sure you will do your best,' he says.

'And that would be your field down there too,' says Joe, pointing over the wall to the field known as the Green Gardens at the top of Tibradden Lane.

'The far one, where the lambs are grazing?' I ask dubiously, for it is not marked as part of our property on the map the solicitor handed me as I left his office, asking me to confirm its accuracy. The map, fluttering like a bird in my hand, shows the entirety of the estate inherited by Charles from his father, extending from the St Thomas lands at Kilmashogue Bridge up over Tibradden Mountain and down into Glencullen. For the most part, the fields are shaded green, indicating they are held under a fee-farm grant in a deed made between Charles Davis and John Jones, on the one part, and the descendants of the Earl of Stafford, the Earl of Cloncarty, Thomas Connolly of Castletown and the Pakenhams of Coolure, on the other, dated 20 September 1851. A fee-farm grant, my father explained, was a peculiarly Irish form of tenure, awarding someone a freehold on the property so long as they continued to pay an annual rent. In this case, he said, after examining the deed, the annual rent was £64 19s. for 118 old Irish acres of lowland and 410 of mountain land. Marymount is shaded brown, held in fee simple from 28 February 1863, meaning the Davis family held this land outright. Very little of the land Charles owned is registered, suggesting it has passed down through title deeds rather than ever having been bought on the open market. The portions he sold off are outlined in red ink, and dated, with the purchaser's name inscribed in red.

Charles sold most of the mountain in 1973, in two lots, one to a neighbouring farmer and the other to the Department for Lands, which turned over the 221 acres to Coillte for forestry. Shooting land, it would have been, for my great-grandfather, Colonel Charles Davis Guinness, to invite his friends over for the Glorious Twelfth when the grouse season traditionally began. Three years later, St Thomas and another hundred acres or so were sold. Smaller sites were sold for the construction of individual houses in the late eighties and early nineties, chipping away here and there at the road frontage.

A tumbledown stone wall divides the field in two: the top half is a wilderness of bracken and gorse, the bottom half grassy pasture. The copse of Scots pine and larch immediately below us glows russet in the sunshine.

'It must be over thirty years I've been grazing the Green Gardens,' Joe says, surveying its bumpy sward. 'That'd be yours now.'

'Well, the trustees',' I say. 'But you'll be going on grazing it for a time yet, Joe, won't you?'

'Oh, I will, if that's all right,' he says, speaking cautiously. 'We have the agreement and all signed with Mr Ganly.'

This, I take it, refers to the eleven-month agreement, drawn up by the estate agent, whereby Joe can graze his own sheep in the Green Gardens. Before Christmas, Charles had called me in to witness his and Susie's signatures on the renewal notice.

'I don't think there will be any changes, at least not for now,' I assure him. Over the wall, the new bracken is beginning to push aside last year's brown stalks. The beeches along Larch Hill's avenue on the other side of the stream form a fresh green canopy. The A-frame of the headquarters at Scouting Ireland pokes discreetly through the trees, like a very solid tepee. Higher still a Coillte plantation of Sitka spruce covers the summit of Kilmashogue in a monochrome green. Looking up the valley, a grove of Lawson cypresses shelters a house and barn beside it, flanked by fields a richer green than the acidic colours of our own. Beyond stretches the heather where the two mountains meet.

'Do you know whose horses those are?' I ask Joe, pointing to a mare and foal grazing on the opposite slope. 'And those fields over there, who do they belong to?'

He regales me with the names of our neighbours and snippets of their history, shaking his head the odd time over some exploit he decides to keep to himself. It is companionable up here, leaning on the wall, listening to Joe talk while Moss, his white sheepdog, sniffs around at our feet. He is a shy man at heart, unsure of himself when telling a tale. On Friday nights, he goes out for a drink at Doherty's; his only leisure as far as I know. I suspect Susie, teetotal all her life, gives him a hard time for it.

I mark the missing field on the map and we get back into Joe's car. Moss jumps into the boot. Joe wants to take me over to his own place in Cruagh, where he keeps his small flock of hoggets on the seven acres he inherited from his mother. He intends to show me the spring he's piped, in case we should ever want to take our own drinking water from it. 'It's sweeter than all that bottled stuff,' he says proudly as we turn down the narrow lane, its entrance marked by a traffic cone jammed onto a post. The track ends at a gated bridge. On the other side of the small stream stands a bungalow. Half of the roof has collapsed, with blackened timbers exposed and tiles sliding off – the house was gutted by fire thirty years ago. Mr Lambert, a neighbouring dairy farmer, spotted the flames when he went out at dawn to collect his cows for milking. He discovered Joe's mother, then an eighty-year-old widow, lying dead on the kitchen floor.

Curtains still hang in the windows. Joe switches off the engine, and I step out into the tall grass.

Charles once pointed out the place high up on Montpelier where Joe grew up in a rudimentary cabin on a relative's farm, 'barely a hut', my uncle said. There seemed to be nothing left of it. This bungalow must have represented a step up in the world for Joe's family. I wonder why he has never attempted to rebuild it.

He leads me through a gate around the side of the house and up the steep bank behind. An open hay shed stands against the far fence, looking incongruously new. He kneels down beside a small box built from loose breeze blocks set into the bank. Breathing hard, he lifts off one of the top blocks to uncover a stopcock and pipe with a reservoir beneath. 'Taste it,' he says, scooping up some water in a plastic cup and handing it to me. I take the cup and drink. The water tastes glacially pure. 'The way I've set it up,' he says, 'stops the sheep from dirtying it. Do you see the trench up there? That's to collect any run-off before it spills into the spring. You just turn the stopcock on and fill up the pool. If you could pipe that out now, you'd make money.'

'You would, Joe,' I say. 'It's delicious.'

He replaces the block and takes me back down to the house.

A pocket garden is fenced off beside the burned-out kitchen. He springs up the bank and wipes his hand on his trousers before extending it to me. I take it, his hand surprisingly strong as he pulls me up, and I step over the wire. Sets of rhubarb are growing lustily among the docks and grass. 'I don't know why it thrives here, but it does,' Joe says. He takes out his penknife and bends down to cut me some stems. They pile up in my arms like sticks of pink holiday rock. 'Susie doesn't care for rhubarb much,' he says, 'but I like it well enough.' I promise to bake him a crumble in exchange.

These seven scrubby acres, all slope and no flat, merely the sunny side of a gully, are the only property Joe owns. Standing beside him as he fills a number of litre bottles from a tap beside the gate, I realize that even if this spring were five miles distant he would still travel to it, for this land and this water are all the birthright he has.

The trustees have asked me to find out the numbers of live-stock held, and the details of any machinery owned, for the probate valuation. They would also welcome a broad picture of how Tibradden will be farmed over the coming year so they can gain some handle on the running costs. The prospect of addressing these questions to Susie fills me with dread.

Our Friday meetings have only become more difficult since Charles died. Susie is broken down with worry that her world will now change, and has given herself over to grief. Each time, I rehearse the same assurances: that the trustees will continue to pay the wages; that the land will still have to be farmed; that the gate-lodge will remain her home. She retrieves a handker-chief from her sleeve and wipes her eyes. 'Ah, poor Master Charles, he could never say no to you,' she concludes often, leaving her hand in mine, the milky pale skin surprisingly soft and smooth beneath the grime. The refrain says as much about her as about Charles. Beyond testifying to my uncle's kindness, what she really means is that Master Charles bowed to her judgement in the management of the farm. By implication, I should too.

This morning, tentatively, I ask Susie for her help in reckoning up our livestock.

'Ah, yes, Miss Selina,' she replies firmly. 'You'd be needing me to tell you how things are done. Of course you would.'

All told, we have twelve cattle – seven bullocks, three heifers and two cows – and a sizeable flock of sheep, counting two rams, sixty-eight ewes, twenty-four hoggets, and the fifty-five lambs that are coming on nicely with the warmer weather and bit of grass. Livestock subsidies are the only direct payments currently claimed from the Department of Agriculture, and these, which don't amount to much, must be transferred into the trustees' names. Tallying the amount of land owned takes longer. Susie names the fields and gives their areas in old Irish acres, which I dutifully write down, realizing only in later conversation with my father that these measurements lost their official status in the nineteenth century. ('Multiply by 1.6 for statute acres,' he'll instruct. 'You'll have to look up the formula for hectares, I'm afraid. That's the agricultural measure.')

As she names the fields and their uses, I realize how differently I know this land. Since I was a child I have walked these same fields not as property or farm, but as landscape, delighting in the curve of the mountain or the line of a hedgerow stretching away from me. I have watched for changes in wind or light. That tree there, grey in shadow a moment ago, now shines silver as the midday haze brightens. I can name the plants and animals, having been schooled early with field guides by my grandmother, and on every walk I continue the game of 'I Spy' we started when I stumbled hand in hand at her side. Occasionally, just to feel the exhilaration of wet, dry, warm, cold, I have closed my eyes to see if my feet can find their own way along the sheep tracks in the grass. In short, I have loved this place as leisure, as childhood, as a natural terrain through which the seasons pass effortlessly, the beauty they create being their chief reward. For Susie, it has been home and employment and livelihood, society and result. The fields may also be to her all that they have been to me; but, free of responsibility, I have sucked on these country pleasures childishly, indulged by the Kirwans' labour.

While Charles was still in hospital, Colin remarked one day how curious it was that Susie still insisted on calling me 'Miss Selina'. I have been trying for years to convince her to drop the embarrassing 'Miss', but in vain. 'Well, then, I should call you not "Susie" but "Mrs Kirwan",' I suggested, when we moved in.

'Ah, not at all, Miss Selina,' she replied, looking genuinely put out. 'There'd be no need for that.'

In the end, Charles advised me to drop the subject, and muttered about old dogs and new tricks. I tended to put Susie's manner of addressing me down to my having retained my maiden name, with 'Mrs Guinness' being reserved in her mind for my grandmother. But Colin disagreed. 'It's more than that. I used to think she used "Master" as a term of respect for Charles because he's her employer, just as your grandfather was "the Major" and your great-grandfather "the Colonel". But I think now it's a totally different term. I reckon she just never changed from the way she addressed him as a boy. He has always been "Master Charles" to her, just as you are "Miss Selina". In her eyes, neither of you has ever really grown up.'

'And then there's the bottom of the Nineteen Acres, what you people always called Marymount,' Susie is saying. 'That's leased in from Major McDowell each year for grazing, as well as the Eleven Acres, which would be the oat field.'

I ask her whether we have much tillage, and if so, what machinery Charles owns. The question raises a chuckle at my naïvety. 'Sure Master Charles doesn't have any machinery. The tractor is Joe's, and anything else belongs to the contractors. Ah, no, with the prices you'd get now for the oats, sure there would be no use in spending money. It would be only throwing good money after bad, Miss Selina, that it would.' For the past four years, the contractor who cuts and bales the silage has taken the tillage fields across the road for 'set-aside'. 'It's when you leave the land idle for the payment from Europe,' Susie explains, in response to my query, shaking her head at the waste. 'There's no sense in it. Noel Plant used to get great barley out of those fields when he had them rented.'

Only the oats remain, and these, according to Susie, were particularly bad last year due to the rain in July. She cannot remember how much was harvested, but because the spray was washed off, the crop was full of weeds and little was got for it. When I ask her whether she thinks it worthwhile growing oats again this year, she is taken aback. 'But what would Johnny Doyle do for feed without it?' For as long as she can remember, a few tonnes have been sold to our neighbour every year, the rest going to the Wicklow Corn Company beyond Rathnew. Other neighbours buy the straw for their horses.

When we have finished, she hauls herself up and says she will walk back down to the lodge. She cannot walk far unaided, and she has only slippers on over her laddered tights. I protest, before I realize that she is not angling for a lift, but instead is determined to demonstrate that she is fit enough to continue at her job. 'You could walk,' I tell her lightly, 'if you want to. But that means I won't get the chance to show off my new car. Please let me drive you down.' She wavers, and then gives in, indulging my whim.

At the lodge, I help her out and up the concrete steps. Joe

opens the door, and can't hide his look of enquiry when he spots me in the porch. 'Goodbye now, Susie,' I call, as she is absorbed into the warm fug of the tiny entry, 'and thank you for your help.' She doesn't hear me over the television. She shouts at Joseph to turn it down before the door is shut and bolted methodically in my wake.

Teagasc, the state agricultural advisory service, sends over their Inspector Morse and Sergeant Lewis to review my case. Morse, or more properly Vincent, is somewhat saturnine; his colleague, Seán, as cheery as the bright May weather. After looking over the maps in the dining room, the two men fetch their gumboots from the car and we go out to walk the land together.

Joe has shorn the sheep in the last day or two, and with their lambs still at foot they look well to my eyes, although I notice the advisers scarcely glance at them. The buttercups are just coming out, turning the Lawn golden, and with the cows mooching from mouthful to mouthful of sweet long grass, and the swallows dipping low over the early summer flies, it is as bucolic an idyll as Constable could ever have painted.

As we walk, Seán encourages me to consider joining REPS, the Rural Environment Protection Scheme. This is a five-year contract with the Department of Agriculture, designed to promote the kind of farming it seems we might already be doing. 'What kind is that?' I ask, raising a faint smile from Vincent as his partner stumbles through a reply.

'Hobby farming,' says Vincent, coming to his aid. He stops, pulls a packet of Marlboro from his pocket and passes one to Seán, from whom he accepts a light. A little crushed, I ask whether a farm of our size and location could ever be viable. He pauses before he speaks. 'As long as you're not hoping to rely on it for your household income, it could be. It all depends on what payments you'd qualify for. Seán is right. You should join REPS for starters; you should also look at planting some of the land with forestry. The key thing for you to find out is what subsidies have been claimed during the past four years, because that's what's going to determine your future income.'

I understand this to be a reference to the Single Farm Payment scheme. Over the past week, my telephone conversations with Teagasc have revealed that I've unwittingly walked in on the quietest revolution in Ireland's recent history. This is the year that the long-promised reform of Europe's Common Agricultural Policy (CAP) comes into full force. Under the new arrangement, farmers will no longer receive direct subsidies for their produce. Instead they will receive a cheque at the end of each year that is based on their stewardship of farmland, regardless of the numbers of livestock owned or the tonnage of crops harvested. The reforms are rooted in the idea that 'decoupling' payments from actual production will end the overproduction of commodities while still providing farmers with a reasonable income. It's really an extension of the set-aside policy, which has required tillage farmers to take 10 per cent of their land out of production, to all other areas of agriculture. Willy Wonka's landscape of wine-lakes and butter-mountains is set to be replaced by a sustainably farmed Arcadia with flora and fauna thriving in fields that were once over-grazed. That is the theory, anyway.

My walk with the two advisers confirms a number of home truths. Our pastures are under-stocked. As Seán puts it, 'The grass is getting ahead of the animals.' The buttercups and the waving seed-heads I admire in the summer months are symptomatic of poor grazing practices. Vincent suspects the oats are making a considerable loss. They inspect the sagging bales of silage stacked up, three high, outside Cloragh. 'You shouldn't have any silage left in May,' says Vincent. 'You're losing money on that.'

In Cloragh farmyard, a kind of depression descends on the two of them. Seán turns over the shards of broken slates with the outside of his boot. 'What will we do about this?' he asks Vincent. Under REPS, he explains, all farmyards are meant to be fitted with drainage systems that separate rainwater from the yard's dirty washings. Gutters need to be kept clear, roofs intact and windows secure. I give a hollow laugh. An elder bush is sprouting through the yawning window above the arched byres where occasionally cattle are still housed. 'It's atmospheric, I'll grant you that,' Seán remarks, as we move through the arch over the cobbles to the lower part of the yard. There's an old hay-barn at the end, its corrugated roof pitted with rust. A rat scutters quickly out of the way. I tell them Joe still uses the pens to our right, and they peer in through the broken-down gates, held together with twine and electrical flex, at the nettles thriving alongside the old dip tub. They exchange a glance.

'Could this be let out to Joe?' Seán asks.

'I suppose so,' I say.

'Well, that might get us out of a hole for REPS,' he says, 'but only for a while.'

Vincent peers inside one of the old sheds. The door is off its hinges. It has been a good few minutes since he said anything at all. I can see him taking in the old farm cart, an abandoned plough, the tractor seat thrown in under a trough over which brambles are growing thick and wild. 'I'll tell you one thing for free,' he finally says, fixing me in the eye. 'You should get out of cattle. You don't have the facilities, and even if you did, raising sucklers on this scale would never make any sense. It never will in Ireland.' If we keep them and sign up to REPS, we will have to fence off access to all water-courses except for designated drinking points. Sheep are a lesser concern because they don't pollute the water in the same way. 'Cut the land you farm in half, and keep the same amount of stock,' he goes on. 'Plant the rest.' Forestry will yield an annual tax-free premium for twenty years. REPS should bring in about seven thousand euros; the main cost will be fencing, for the whole farm has to be stock-proof by the end of year one.

We return to the house. Their immediate concern is that Charles has never submitted an Area Aid application for the farm, hence missing out on subsidies to which he would have been entitled. All payments to farmers until 2013 are going to be based on the information collected on this year's Area Aid forms. In Tibradden's case, the lack of any prior application means there is much catching up to be done before the forms can be filled in. The closing date for 2004 was 31 March. If I can prove our application has been delayed by *force majeure*, I have until 1 July. If I don't make the deadline, I'll have missed the boat on payments, not for this year alone but for the next decade.

Given that Charles's entitlements are likely to be of very low value, Vincent advises me to apply to the National Reserve Fund. From what I can understand, this is a kind of hard-luck pot into which the Department of Agriculture throws a percentage of the total agricultural budget allocated to Ireland through the CAP annually. These funds will be redistributed as new entitlements among those who inherited land over the past three years, or those who have taken up farming this year. The trustees will have to authorize the Department of Agriculture to transfer Charles's herd number into my name. 'I often say that if I were going to dances now, chance would be a fine thing, I'd be as likely to ask a girl for her herd number as her phone number,' Seán jokes.

We will also have to decide within the next fortnight what to do about the fields rented in and the land leased out for set-aside. 'I am sorry to put you under pressure,' says Vincent, 'but the farm has to be digitally mapped and an identification number assigned to each land parcel on our information system before we can sign off on the application. Now is the time to make up your mind whether you want to keep farming or not.'

I sink my head into my hands. Although I am confident that with Teagasc's help we will be able to submit the paperwork in time, I don't relish trying to explain all this to Susie. It will also be a challenge to persuade the two besuited trustees who officially own the livestock that these decisions cannot wait until after probate. Their instructions were to try to keep Tibradden going without change in circumstance until the land has been legally transferred; but it is clear from what Seán and Vincent have said that, if we don't make various changes needed to qualify for the Single Farm Payment and to enter REPS and avail of other support mechanisms, the long-term viability of the farm is in doubt. We have a fortnight to decide the future of Tibradden.

Vincent and Seán have suggested that the first step towards a REPS application is to compile a flock register. This involves bringing in the sheep and recording their tag numbers on a single day. Subsequently all deaths, sales and purchases can be entered in the register.

Joe is sceptical about the value of this exercise, but agrees to humour me. By the time Colin and I arrive down in the yard, he has divided the sheep into two batches, the ewes in the pens and the hoggets confined to the bottom section next to the hay-barn. Outside the pens, the lambs are bleating desperately; their mothers butt each other aside in the fight to comfort them.

Joe suggests that Colin climb into the pens with him. He

will catch and hold each sheep, so that Colin can read off the tag number for my book. I station myself at the big oil barrel beside them, pen at the ready.

It has to be said that my husband did not welcome the prospect of helping Joe today, grumbling that he has yet to recover from helping Joe get the cattle in earlier this week for their TB test. This involved herding twelve large cows into a small windowless outhouse, about the size of a single bedroom, at the corner of the upper yard. Once inside, Joe closed the door behind them. The cattle milled about, their panic setting the dark in motion. 'They'll move towards the light,' Joe called, as he lifted the latch and, to Colin's great dismay, stepped out. Colin's task was to catch hold of the cows one by one and shoulder them out through a ragged gap in the wall and into the cattle-crush fixed on the other side. There Joe would lock each beast in place by sliding an iron bar quickly beneath its hindquarters before it could back out. Colin did his best, but despite the protection of steel-toed hiking boots he couldn't help feeling that both the vet and Joe were underestimating the novice's fear of being trapped in a room with twelve stampeding animals, each five or six times his weight and seemingly twice as nifty in the dark.

That night he displayed the bruises up and down his shins without heroism. 'Vincent was right,' he said, 'we should get out of cattle. Sheep are smaller.'

The ewes, though certainly smaller, prove equally resistant to capture. Joe spreads his arms and advances sideways, a good-natured crab, quietly coaxing all the time. Most allow him to slip his arm swiftly around their head and grip them by the chin so that Colin can read out the numbers on their ear tags. A few dodge past Joe, causing Colin to lunge and grab. I try hard not to laugh as he is dragged round the pen by one ewe, desperately clinging to her tail. 'Ah, that one's pure-bred

Cheviot,' Joe consoles him, as he picks himself up. 'They can be a bit wild, all right.' Colin does not seem to be enjoying the humiliation. I can see him questioning how he came to be living this life.

There are fifty-one ewes in all, including two without tags. This is seventeen fewer than the figure Susie gave me, leading me to wonder whether we have lost so many ewes during lambing, or whether Susie's memory was inaccurate. 'Does that hurt?' I ask Joe, as he punches a tag through a sheep's left ear.

'No, they don't seem to mind,' he answers. The ewe contradicts him by shaking her head vigorously. 'Ask your good husband there if his hurt.'

'What's that?' Colin asks, and I grip my own earlobe between forefinger and thumb and waggle it. 'Oh.' A rueful smile softens his expression as he reaches up to twist the thin silver ring. 'I'd forgotten I still have it in.'

It takes a couple of hours to get through the entire flock, hoggets included. The lambs won't be tagged until they are weaned. We would get through it faster, I realize, if Joe wasn't dependent on Colin to read out the tag numbers. It begins to dawn on me that Joe's eyesight is not the problem: rather, he lacks confidence in his own ability to read the tags. The few times he tries, he asks one of us to push through to the back of the pen and confirm he has the number right. He confuses sixes and nines. At first, I assume this is a natural error as the sheep mill about, but then it occurs to me that the only thing I've ever seen Joe write is his own name on the dockets that accompanied some of our cattle to mart. When he brought me the cattle passports that day, he asked me to read out loud the ages inscribed on them. I assumed he was checking whether his wife's handwriting was legible to others, and did so, but I now realize he was probably squaring this information against his recollections of calving them and doing some mental calculation on that basis. From the way he leaned on the biro at the place I indicated for his signature, from the care he took, I should have known that reading and writing presented a challenge.

All over Ireland, there must be men like Joe for whom working with livestock once meant freedom from paperwork and the impossible standards it set. You reared a beast, took it to mart, sold it and put some money by to purchase a replacement. But since agricultural policy has been governed by Europe, paperwork has been at the heart of profitable farming. No matter how hard you work in the fields, or how good you are with animals, livestock sales no longer make up the bulk of farm incomes. While Susie has been able to fill in the forms for subsidies and direct payments, Joe has been able to farm without revealing his illiteracy to anyone. But at the age of eighty, and with her failing eyesight, there must be some question as to how long Susie can continue to do this for both of them. In Friday's talk of flock registers and REPS plans, Area Aid applications and stocking quotas, they must feel the jaws of officialdom tightening on their lives. I am beginning to understand now why Charles couldn't face talking about the farm.

8.

June 2004

The crocodile sits inside the door, on guard. The estate agent, valuer and insurance broker troop in through the hall and out again, marking the progress of the world that Charles can no longer keep at bay. As if it somehow knew that he would not return, the house itself appears to have given up holding out for him, and decides instead to let its vital organs finally succumb to old age. One night, watching television from the sofa next to Charles's empty chair, I hear the sudden sound of water rushing through the central-heating pipes. It doesn't stop. I run to the basement and discover a fountain gushing through the glass eye of the boiler where the furnace used to burn. The floor is already several inches deep in red, rusty, filthy-smelling water.

The repairman is astonished when he arrives to survey the damage: 'My goodness, a ship's boiler – this must date from the 1930s.' He displays the corroded parts in frank amazement that a house this size can have been heated by such a piece of machinery for so long. The boiler's disintegration is followed by the water tank's, prompting a second deluge in the basement; then the flashing along the roof's central valley cracks and the rain floods in through the skylight and on down to the hall below. The ark we inhabit seems so poorly tarred that I find it hard to believe it will survive the indeterminate spell the trustees have decreed we must sail before we find dry land after probate. No significant work, they said. When I ask the roofer to patch and repair, he shakes his head. The central valley should slope gently towards the external gutters, but instead slopes in towards the skylight, ensuring the rain drains through it during the summer storms. I should also know, he continues, that the chimney wobbled when he brushed against it.

I inform the trustees of these events, and they encourage me to do the minimum necessary to keep the house habitable. This does not extend to installing a new central-heating system, or rebuilding the roof.

I spend the wet days on the floor of the study, searching amid the flotsam of five generations for the missing share certificates the trustees have bade me find. I expect Charles's most important documents to have washed up here, for the study has traditionally been the place where estate business has been conducted. I find a few envelopes with 'Important' scrawled across the front in red biro, the word underlined twice, before being chucked among the rest on the weary sofa. They are empty. I find an ESB bill from the 1930s and briefly consider its historical worth, before bending to the task of sifting through letters from the same firms of estate agents, valuers and insurers called in by the executors for my grandfather thirty-three years ago. A refuse sack bulges beside me like a huge black toad. The room is dark, despite the overhead light. The top sash on the far window has finally given way so the shutters must remain closed against the rain. When I look up, I catch my reflection in the clouded mirror of the bookcase door, and note how two-dimensional I appear against the tobacco-coloured walls. The model of the forty-two-pound salmon caught by Lord Massy at Hermitage on the Shannon in 1887 (according to the inscription) appears more real, swimming off into the recesses of the room, while I am the specimen, landed out of my element.

Yesterday, watching the valuer glide from room to room,

inspecting objects and returning them just slightly out of place, I understood for the first time that these interiors are all fit-ups, stages set for the play and business of each generation. The crocodile does not have to be forever stationed at our front door; the games chest with its cache of cracked cricket bats and stumps could be heaved downstairs or overboard altogether. And yet this furniture, wood-wormed and ring-stained as it is, arranged as I remember it, provides the ballast of the house, anchoring stories to it that might otherwise float away. If Tibradden and its contents are bequeathed to me, then the challenge will be to work out what service this past can perform, to find a form of stewardship that will not stifle our future.

Behind the central mirrored door of the study bookcase lies the map store. Most of the maps are scrolled loosely; some, backed in linen, are folded flat into packets and bound with pink legal tape; others are rolled onto wooden poles, one or two with their leather cases intact. They all show signs of use, marked and torn from being spread out on tables and smoothed by various hands. The large-scale Ordnance Survey maps have suffered most, as Charles has simply cut from them whatever site maps were required for deeds of sale. Spread out on the square of maroon carpet I have cleared, they resemble patterns for a dress with elaborate pleats and seams.

One linen map unrolls to show the neighbouring townlands of Killakee, James's Land and Cruagh, the estate of Luke White Esq., surveyed by William Duncan in 1806. The hillocks and declivities are shaded in pencil, the fields outlined in ink, so that the land appears all elbows and armpits, streams, tracks and avenues running through it like veins. The tenants' names are inscribed in each field along with their areas, given in the old measure of acres, roods and perches. I locate the stream I recently crossed with Joe and find his stepfather's family name, Murphy, inscribed on his slope of a field. Doyle, Casey, Magrath and Kavanagh are among Mr Murphy's neighbours, the names familiar from Friday's conversations with Susie. Two hundred years later, these families are still farming the same land, seven miles from the centre of Dublin.

My grandmother always explained to visitors that, contrary to their expectations, Tibradden had not been built with brewery money: 'My husband's family were all church mice.' Although Thomas Hosea Guinness was the great-grandson of the legendary Arthur Guinness, the first brewer and lessor of St James's Gate in Dublin, Arthur's eldest son, Hosea, took up holy orders in the Church of Ireland. The Reverend Hosea Guinness, of St Werburgh's parish, behind Dublin Castle, persuaded his eldest son, Arthur, to follow suit. By the time Thomas came along, any worldly wealth in the senior branch of the Guinness family had been given up to the glory of God. Thomas was a practising solicitor in church law when he married Mary Davis, then twenty-eight years old. She was a good catch.

The Davises lived at Cloragh, an attractive Georgian farmhouse with substantial out-offices laid out in three distinct yards behind the house; the ruins of these buildings and yards now serve as our untidy and derelict farmyard. When Mary Davis married Thomas Hosea Guinness in 1859, her father, Charles Davis, built a house for the couple as a wedding present on the site of another Georgian farmhouse just up the avenue. The new Tibradden, designed by the Dublin architect Joseph Maguire, was a much grander building than its predecessor. The hall floor was laid with Minton encaustic tiles in umber, slate grey and cream in a pattern to mirror the ornately Corinthian plasterwork on the ceiling. A pair of marble pillars and a stained-glass window completed the fashionably Gothic effect. Plate-glass was used for the big picture windows in the drawing room and dining room. Tibradden's grandeur would have made Cloragh seem plain and old-fashioned by comparison.

Mary Davis knew she was to be her father's heir from the age of fourteen, when the last of her three brothers died. Her mother, also called Mary, had died young, so the daughter had grown up alone with her father, in what my uncle always considered the dark and gloomy environment of Cloragh. According to my own father, the title deeds reveal that Charles Davis inherited Cloragh from his mother, Sarah, and purchased the Tibradden property from a cousin, John Jones, in 1851. In addition, a large farm in Carlow, bought by Charles's father in the late 1700s, would be left to Mary's eldest son when he attained his majority at twenty-one. My uncle told me once that the only legend he could recall of my great-great-grandmother's character was that some visitor who dared to admire the prospect from her new front steps had been roundly rebuked with the words, 'I am heartily sick of it.' I wonder now how long her family had been staring down at the city.

Ostensibly I am looking for a map the estate agent can use to value the farm, but really I'm more curious to discover the cartographical skeleton beneath our land. The earliest map I can find of this property is one titled 'Clora Estate', commissioned by Mrs Sarah Davis in 1811 from a surveyor named James Byrne. It is a delicate and pretty thing, with pictorial representations of buildings and vegetation; the fields are washed in aquamarine, the trunks of trees finely drawn in brown and grey inks, topped with tiny explosions of bottle-green foliage. Some of the trees cast tiny shadows to the north, as if James Byrne had set up his theodolite late one summer's afternoon and decided to record the declining heat of the day; as if the shimmer in his sights were as much part of the landscape as the land itself. A short avenue runs straight up to the semi-circular sweep in front of the house; a gate-lodge is positioned at its entrance, halfway down Cloragh Road.

This building has since been knocked down and replaced by a two-winged mansion set back from the road, but I remember my grandmother taking me across the lawn to visit Mrs Nolan there. We'd feed her donkeys sugar cubes and take tea in her tiny parlour, and on the way back my grandmother used to tell me how we had to thank the Nolans for our water supply. It was Tom Nolan who'd laid the pipes carrying the stream down from Larch Hill on the instructions of my great-grand-uncle, Ernest, who was an engineer. Without him, she said, we'd still be ferrying water in buckets.

A pretty picture of Cloragh has been drawn in pen and ink in the upper right-hand corner of the map. I have to struggle hard to match this elegant Georgian house to the ruined shell I know. It has two windows either side of the fan-lighted front door, five windows above, a chimney-stack at either end. This symmetry continues in the pair of arches positioned either side of the house, leading on the right into the rear yard, where Joe continues to house the cattle in the old byres, and on the left to a small plantation, now overgrown. The plantation is divided into three sections with pathways in between – pleasure grounds, perhaps even then planted up with the black walnut, now split at the bole, and the holm oak at its end.

The plantation's southern field boundary runs in a continuous line down to the stream, named here as the Marymount River. I recall Susie's words when we were tallying the land – 'The Nineteen Acres, what you people always called "Marymount"' – and it strikes me how close this history still is. I wonder if one of these watercolour trees with their exploding foliage might not be the lime tree in the centre of the Lawn. It's hard to find my bearings without it, though I can see that the Lawn, now one large field of about twelve acres, is here divided in four, the lower three parts belonging to Cloragh, the upper assigned to 'Tibradin' Demesne.

Mrs Sarah Davis must have been a widow to have held this land in her own right in 1811. Until the Married Women's Property Act in 1882, the common law of coverture ruled that any property inherited by a woman automatically passed to her husband upon marriage. On this map, at least, Cloragh's demesne looks small. I size it up against the aerial photographs of these same acres the Department of Agriculture sent me earlier this week. From these images, so pixellated that it is hard in places to discern the boundary between our fields and our neighbours', the department will calculate the precise area I will be allowed to claim under the new Single Farm Payment scheme. Tracts of scrub and bracken, copses, bushy hedgerows and wherever else it may be difficult for animals to graze have to be deducted from their calculation. James Byrne's map is more attractive than the blurry photos, expressing as it does the grace and favour of the landscape, the park planted with spreading trees for shade and timber, but I suspect it was commissioned under a similar set of circumstances: the rattle of earth on a coffin as the body becomes ground, the rustle of paper as ground becomes property.

Among the maps is a large roll of white card. Thinking it's some poster drawn up by my grandmother for one of her pantomimes, I open it prepared to toss it aside. I'm amazed to discover a Davis family tree I've never seen before. Charles spent many evenings trying to interest me in how I was related to various distant cousins by opening up 'the Guinness studbook', as my mother disparagingly called it, and flicking from page to page while I did my best to follow him down the road of once and twice and three times removeds. He must have consulted this tree, for the card shows signs of wear and tear and the occasional impatient question mark is pencilled in his handwriting next to entries, but he never showed it to me.

The genealogist was my great-grand-uncle Ernest Guinness, who signed and dated it in 1895. The bottom line records the birth of my grandfather, Owen, and his older brother, Hugh Spencer, whose early death in 1922 is the last date to be recorded. Ernest must have kept working at it over the years, entering the deaths of his younger brothers and sisters, and lastly of his nephew, eleven years before his own. It seems appropriate that the man responsible for engineering our water supply should also have charted the passage of blood down through the tributaries into this delta of Davis cousins fanning out across the page. All descend from John and Anne Davis of Murphystown, County Dublin: John, who wrote his will in 1683, the first document in a series of wills and title deeds in which, my father tells me, lies much of the information I am seeking.

Here is Mrs Sarah Davis, *née* Jones, married on St Valentine's Day 1790, at the age of nineteen, to James Moore Davis, a man sixteen years her senior. He is the great-great-grandson of the first John Davis and heir to the farm at Murphystown. I have to squint hard to make out the words 'printer and gentleman' inscribed against his name. I like the combination. Together they had five children, two of whom survived to marry and bear grandchildren. Sarah was made a widow in 1800, three years after the birth of her last child, a boy, named James like his father. She was probably living then on the farm at Murphystown, where the extension of the Luas green line is set to run through to Bride's Glen. The entry for Eleanor Moore, her mother-in-law, adds 'from a respectable family possessed of a city estate', a boast somewhat undercut by the plainer designation 'joiner', pencilled in next to Eleanor's father's name. In early Georgian Dublin, joiners must have profited from the housing boom that gave the city its gracious squares.

James Moore Davis's elder brother, named John after his father and great-great-grandfather, also married a Jones – Mary, Sarah's older sister. Against her name is written in tiny letters, 'married at 15, a husband 15 years older, bore him 15 children'. I stop to consider this. The two brothers, John and James, had paired off with two sisters, Sarah and Mary, the daughters of Charles Jones Esq. He is described here as a 'provider', that is a general goods purveyor, of Killincarrig, Delgany, County Wicklow. John and James's sister, Sussannah Davis, was married off to their immediate neighbour, Robert Marchbank of Prospect Lodge, a mere step away across Cloragh Road.

I have to track back a generation to find mention of Cloragh and Tibradden. They are first listed as properties in the possession of their father's younger brother, Richard Davis, 1725–1809. He had four children, only one of whom, Anne, had issue. She is listed as the 'heiress of Tibradden', the wife of James Jones, a clothier of Brabazon Row, Dublin. Scanning across Anne's generation, I realize that of the six first cousins who married, three appear to have married Joneses. It seems reasonable to presume that Anne's husband, James, was a brother to Mary and Sarah Jones. The trades named on this family tree – printer, clothier, weaver, joiner – suggest that, in the eighteenth century, the Davises were modest enough tenant farmers to require regular off-farm wages.

When Richard Davis died in 1809, he left his farmhouse at Tibradden to his daughter Anne, and bequeathed Cloragh to his niece by marriage, Sarah Davis, née Jones. And so she must have arrived some time around 1811: a forty-year-old widow, with four children in tow, the youngest aged fourteen. With her brother up the avenue (presuming James was a brother), and her sister at Eden Park, a pleasant walk away through the La Touche estate at Marlay, her two eldest boys, John and

Charles Davis, then aged twenty and eighteen, would have entered a close-knit society with sixteen first cousins as their near neighbours. When it came time for Charles to marry in 1829, he chose the youngest of his aunt's surviving daughters at Eden Park. Aged twenty-five, Mary was nine years his junior and his first cousin on both the maternal and paternal sides. With seven surviving elder siblings, it may be that the pool of suitors had run dry by the time she came of age, but this is closely wed by any reckoning.

The white marble monuments in Whitechurch, mourning the loss of sons who died as officers in the dragoons during the Boer War, suggest that Mary's family, the Moore-Davises at Eden Park off the Grange Road, were the wealthier branch, able to buy commissions in the fashionable regiments, perhaps with the revenue from Eleanor's 'city estate'. The farms attached to Cloragh and Tibradden stretched beyond their immediate demesnes, but not far: the total land amounted to 188 statute acres of lowland grazing, and 656 statute acres of mountain heath. From the evidence of James Byrne's map and this family tree, the Davises of Cloragh and the Joneses of Tibradden, although comparatively well heeled, would have stood together at the edge of the Pale, as the Bennetts not the Darcys of their world.

Charles and Mary were not the only cousins to marry, although they were certainly the closest. Of the seven children raised by Anne Jones at Tibradden, the only two to marry also married relatives: Eliza wed her second cousin, Richard Davis; Eliza's brother, John Jones, wed Mary Marchbank, old Sussannah Davis's grand-daughter and his own second cousin once removed. Elsewhere, too, the same names recur as marriage partners through the generations: Richardsons and Murphys feature regularly in addition to the Joneses. I am curious whether this interbreeding among cousins helped to consolidate the transfer of property within the family, or whether it is simply an indication of how tight a circle existed among this class of Protestant farmers.

When I track back through the generations to try to figure out how Cloragh passed down to Charles Davis, I consider how odd it is that his great-uncle Richard chose not to leave this property to any of his own four children. Instead, in 1811, he bequeathed it to Charles's mother, Sarah, his niece-by-marriage. While Richard's daughter Anne inherited Tibradden, no property is appended to the entries for her two sisters, Sussannah and Eleanor. His son, unnamed, survived long enough to marry but appears to have predeceased his father without leaving children. If Richard was concerned that Cloragh should remain in the Davis family, perhaps Sussannah and her husband, William Richardson, were discounted as childless and of an age beyond child-bearing.

This still leaves Richard's other daughter, his third-born, Eleanor. When I look at her again, I notice that a very faint note has been pencilled in underneath her name, the words carefully enclosed in inverted commas: 'who behaved herself grossly'. There is no exclamation mark to indicate amusement, just this bare verdict recorded on a factual family tree: Eleanor, D.S.P. (*decessit sine prole*, died without issue), behaved herself grossly. What on earth was her crime? I smooth out the card again and try to calculate when she lived. There are no dates of birth or death recorded for her, but her father married Elizabeth Luke on 11 July 1752. As the third child, Eleanor was likely born towards the latter end of the decade.

It seems reasonable to assume Richard Davis raised his family at Tibradden, since it precedes Cloragh as the first of the two properties inscribed against his name. This means Eleanor would have grown up here, not in these rooms, but in the earlier L-shaped farmhouse that stood on this site. For a moment,

I let go of the chart and try to imagine the layout of the house as it was then: a narrower building, judging from one of the maps, with chimney stacks at either end, like Cloragh, a flagged entrance hall with wooden stairs rising to the bedrooms, a fanlight over the front door. Darker, busier with work, the walled garden used for growing vegetables: I picture the constant toings and froings of people with all manner of implements and occupations. This study at the rear of the house could have been a study then, too, for it sits directly above the kitchen where we exposed the windows of the original farmhouse during our renovations. Has this room always been a male preserve, a place where a father might come to contemplate his daughter's gross behaviour?

Somewhere, furled in the cubby-holes of the writing desk by the window, or its bottom drawers, or among my great-grandfather's diaries, there might be some further clue. These documents should be set aside for investigation at a later date, once the pressing estate business is resolved. Yet now that I have begun to comb through them I find it impossible to stop searching for an end to this story.

'CUIMNIG, the Irish characters on Mary Guinness's bracelet signify – REMEMBER.' This is the first sentence in the small purple notebook, dog-eared and soft-covered, that I find buried beneath the maps on the bottom shelf. Its title – 'Traditions, Stories, etc.' – glistens like sea glass to my greedy eye. My great-grandfather, Colonel Charles Davis Guinness, filled just the first seven of its yellow pages with information for the family record. I skim through the unhappy tale of Queen Gormlaí, whose third marriage to Niall Darragh of Glendhu, the King of Ulster, ended with his death in battle against the Norsemen of Dublin on the battlefields of Kilmashogue in AD 919. 'According to Mike Keogh of Kilmashogue,' writes the Colonel, 'Niall is the king buried on top of Tibradden Mountain. Queen Gormlaí met her death through falling in her sleep on a bed-stick which pierced her heart whilst dreaming she saw her [dead] King.' This last detail is attributed to Dr George Siger-son's antiquarian classic *Bards of the Gael and Gall*, which dates these reminiscences to some time after 1897.

At the far side of Marymount, there is a semi-circular ditch topped with trees. I had thought it a prehistoric fort, but now I wonder whether it isn't the remains of the chieftain's redoubt. Marymount is a broad sweep of a field, softly sloping towards the city, the last natural plain before the hillsides close in at Larch Hill. If Niall's forces had gathered here, they could have watched King Sitric's Norsemen approaching up the valley from Rathfarnham. I remember now the day last summer when I walked the field with a film location scout who tutted at the electricity poles cutting across what he described as an otherwise perfect battlefield. We stopped talking for a moment to imagine an army assembled on horses, the thunder of hoofs.

The Colonel's next entry skips forward a cool nine hundred years:

> During the Rebellion in 1798, the rebels came to Cloragh and demanded arms. No one was in except Miss Davis, daughter of Richard Davis. She said she had only one gun. She handed it out to the rebels, muzzle foremost. 'Take it back,' said the rebels, 'and hand it out stock foremost.' She did so. They went looking everywhere for arms and met Mr. PROSSER, a farmer, they pursued him to Cloragh hall door, where they shot him dead. He had been out shooting rabbits on his own land.

Unless the Colonel wrote 'Miss' in error, it must have been Eleanor – the only spinster left among Richard's three daugh-ters by 1798 – who opened the door to the rebels. I wonder was

it late in 1798, or earlier in the year. News of the sectarian kill-
ings in Wexford may have reached her ears; perhaps she had
even heard of the massacre at Scullabogue in May, when the
rebels herded Protestant men, women and children into a
barn, locked the doors and set it alight, piking those who
escaped. I imagine her terror as she handed over the gun and
her humiliation at her fumbling, at being told she had got this
wrong. When the men left to search for arms elsewhere, they
would have gone up Cloragh Road towards Prossers'. In their
wake, did she leave the house and run up the avenue to Tibradden? Or did she shoot home the bolts and look for somewhere
to hide? Was she there when Mr Prosser came running to her
door to seek refuge? Did she struggle to admit him, or was she
too terrified to go to his aid? I wonder was Mr Prosser shot
with the very gun she had surrendered. As her neighbour died
on her doorstep, did she think she was to blame?

The rebels' raid was a bold one. Less than half a mile away
at Killakee, battalions of the British Army congregated in
Stocking Lane to buy provisions for the long march over the
newly built Military Road across the boggy Featherbed and
down into the glens of west Wicklow, thick with hazel and
alder, where Michael Dwyer and his men evaded capture long
after the defeats of Wexford and Mayo. In these upper reaches
of Rathfarnham, soldiers and rebels must have criss-crossed
constantly. Our valley served as a back door to Dublin for the
Wicklow men. John Philpot Curran, the attorney for the
United Irishmen who defended Wolfe Tone and Hamilton
Rowan, lived behind Whitechurch in a house called The Priory.
His daughter, Sarah Curran, would woo her sweetheart, the
doomed rebel leader Robert Emmet, in the grounds of
Hermitage opposite, where Pádraig Pearse's school, St Enda's,
would later be housed. In 1803, when Emmet's uprising failed,
he escaped briefly through this area into the high wastes of the

Dublin Mountains, assisted by Sarah and his loyal servant, Anne Devlin.

I turn the page. Sarah Davis, too, witnessed the violence of the rebellion on a drive into Dublin with her sister and mother, 'in a covered car with a feather bed inside. When passing St Stephen's Green their mother, Mrs Jones of Killincarrig, saw the rebels hanging at the corner of the Square and told her daughters not to look. They of course looked out and saw the corpses hanging.'

The Colonel's next anecdote comes from his own childhood, and recounts how he and his siblings were driven into town from Tibradden to take refuge in the Shelbourne Hotel during the Fenian Rising of 1867. His father, Thomas Hosea Guinness, remained at home and led a battalion of the Scots Greys over the hill and through the woods in pursuit of the fleeing rebels after the Battle of Tallaght. He captured one of them, the infamous James Fitzharris, a.k.a. 'Skin the Goat', in Millikins' field, or Marymount, and later released him. A note at the foot of the page records that in 1882 'Skin the Goat' would drive the Phoenix Park Murderers away from their assassination scene, leaving the chief secretary, Lord Frederick Cavendish, and his under-secretary, T. H. Burke, to die of their stab wounds.

In his last entry, the Colonel returns to Cloragh, as if some loose thread remained to be pulled.

Old (Dick) Richard Davis built Cloragh House and left Cloragh to Sarah Davis (no blood relation to him). She was Miss Jones of Killincarrig. Her son, John Davis of Eden Park, Rathfarnham, built the range of [farm] offices at Cloragh.

He (John) was very fond of hunting and on one occasion had his red coat spoilt by dirty water thrown over him out of the window of the Long Room at Cloragh by a sister of Sarah Davis, who was a bit queer and who was kept more or less a prisoner in the room beyond the Long Room at Cloragh. This lady had a craze for not wearing any clothes!

Whereas every other tale in the Colonel's notebook describes the Davises' domestic world as imperilled by wider political events, the dirtying of John's hunting coat by a madwoman locked in the room above reveals the turbulence at home. Could the madwoman have been Eleanor, who, according to the family tree, 'behaved herself grossly'? Although the Colonel identifies the woman who spoiled John Davis's coat as Sarah's sister, it seems possible that the Colonel's mother, from whom he would have had the story, wished to distance such behaviour from the Davis bloodline – and Sarah was a Jones. It seems to me probable that the unnamed woman who figures in both of the Colonel's reminiscences of Cloragh is Eleanor – and that Eleanor may be the key to the mystery of why Richard Davis, having bequeathed Tibradden to one of his daughters, left Cloragh not to either of the other two but to his niece by marriage, Sarah. If, as these scraps of family history suggest, Eleanor was to some degree mad or wayward, the question of who might care for her must have weighed heavily on Richard's mind as he drafted his will. Sarah, though not of his blood, had been a widow for a long while, and her own children were nearly reared. Perhaps, along with the house and the small demesne, Sarah inherited the burden of caring for Eleanor.

An old photograph shows Cloragh intact, its façade covered with ivy, a group of children standing awkwardly to the left of the front door. I had presumed it a straightforward house with two or three bedrooms above two front parlours, but a neighbour who knew the house in childhood tells me that a series of returns broke up the two flights of stairs leading to smaller bedrooms for children, a nursery, and pantries in the basement. What the Colonel called the 'Long Room' in his notebook, she says, was the room above the back kitchen – the short stroke of the L in the house's original structure.

I let myself into the farmyard through the black pitch door next to the kitchen and stand in the covered area. Joe told me once it was designed for carts to back into and unload their goods at the kitchen door without getting wet. The yard is deserted; the only sound I hear is Moss moving around on her straw. Cloragh's grassy cobbles are littered with broken slates and flitters of silage wrap in the corners. A wood-pigeon flies in under the arch and settles on a board that flaps free from the rafter at its farthest end. Her nest is positioned unwisely at the top of this gangplank. This is the second spring her eggs have rolled down it as they hatched, smashing onto the stones below.

Cloragh has been derelict for as long as I can remember, with its roof caved in and an ash tree growing up through what would have been the hall. The spokes of the fanlight above the hall door where Mr Prosser was shot have become detached from their frame, like a broken bicycle wheel. The rear wall, with the outline of an arched window similar to the one at Tibradden, stands free from its corner stones. It seems to teeter – one small push would be enough to bring it down.

I call for Joe and, hearing no answer, open the door on my right to the back kitchen. It is a low room, its floor scattered with straw and its rafters exposed. A discarded sofa is piled high with plastic sacks of feed, their contents leaking from the holes chewed by rats. An old range, built into the wall, still has an iron kettle placed on the hob. In front of me a set of plain wooden stairs rises up to the next floor. Fearful of rats, I make my way up.

The 'Long Room' is unexpectedly bright and airy, for where the top sash has given way, the morning sun falls long and full onto an iron bedstead hauled into the centre of the room. A rusty red ochre is dusted on the walls, softening the light again. At the top of the stairs a linen press is recessed into the wall. Its limed doors stand ajar as if awaiting sheets dried on the line and freshly ironed. A little anteroom opens off to my left where this back wing joins onto the main house. Inside is a barred door. If I unlocked it and went through, I would step into thin air where the landing used to be. At the far end of the room is another door. I tentatively pick my way towards it, mindful of the rotten rafters on view below. I test its handle, then put my shoulder against it reluctantly, but the door remains closed.

Eleanor's room, where, in the Colonel's words, she was 'kept more or less a prisoner', was 'beyond the Long Room'. If I were Sarah, taking up residence in 1811, I'd have chosen this Long Room for a sitting room where I could invite Eleanor to join me when she was feeling well. What kind of threshold did the door at the far end, a perfectly ordinary panelled door, present for each of Cloragh's occupants? Not knowing what else to do, I sit down on the iron bedstead and try to imagine the two of them here together before rising to descend the stairs.

9.

September 2004

In the autumn I learn from the trustees that they intend to appoint Tibradden to me. The relief is immense. I feel as if the string from which I've been dangling since Charles's death has finally been cut and I am on solid ground again. It seems that my brother and my father separately and generously explained to the trustees that they, like Charles, wanted Tibradden to remain in the family and that I was the only family member prepared to take on the work of living here. The nightmare I feared was not the thought of moving again and building our lives elsewhere, but that of seeing Tibradden sold and, inevitably, turned into something completely different. With this fear removed, Colin and I can at last relax and call Tibradden our home.

Despite the work Colin has put in with Joe down in the yard, he has tended to hold back in matters of farm business, leaving me to meet my Teagasc consultants and work out how to implement their advice, while keeping the Kirwans onside. Over the summer, what I perceived to be his lack of interest led to arguments. I felt overwhelmed by the number of decisions I had to take to secure the future of a place in which we yet had no security. I was impatient and ratty, perhaps because I feared that Colin resented the weight of responsibilities settling down around us just one year into our marriage. Farming had never figured in his plans for the future and yet here I was, night after night, trying to comprehend the different agricultural schemes that would make farming an intrinsic part of both our lives.

The trustees' announcement allows us finally to talk openly about our future. I was wrong, he tells me, to have mistaken his withdrawal for reluctance about living here and all the work it would entail. What I have to understand is that whereas I consider the fields mine to walk, he has felt as if he were trespassing on territory that more properly belonged to other men: my uncle, the trustees, my father and Joe.

'But if you're my husband,' I protest, 'it is yours too. I need to know that you are content for Tibradden to become not just our home, but our lives.'

'But that question was answered long ago,' he says, 'long before we came to live here. Our first night together you spoke of Charles and Kitty and what Tibradden meant to you. So how on earth could I refuse to live here with you now?'

Now that Tibradden is ours, his reservations about his role here have diminished. His reassurance feels like a renewal of our marriage vows. Neither of us is under any illusion about the tasks ahead. We still have no heating, a leaking roof and a hazardous electricity supply, none of which can be repaired until after the estate has cleared probate, the property is formally conveyed and we obtain a mortgage. Indoors, outdoors, wherever we turn, there are things to repair or replace or ditch in a skip. Nor are we sure yet what the inheritance tax bill is likely to be or how we will pay it. But as both of us are lucky enough to enjoy permanent lectureships within a reasonable commuting distance, Colin having recently moved from Queen's to Maynooth, it seems plausible to assume we will survive somehow.

The trustees are practical men, and one of the factors in their decision to appoint me heir to Tibradden is that, unlike my father and brother, I qualify for 'agricultural relief' on the inheritance tax, calculated on the market value of the land at the date of Charles's death: a discount of 90 per cent. Now, to settle the tax bill, we require a valuation of the entire property.

I had thought naïvely that this would be a relatively straightforward task. Tibradden retained its agricultural zoning under the most recent Dun Laoghaire/Rathdown County Development Plan, so I assumed our fields could be valued on the basis of the current price for agricultural land around here. The estate agent soon set me right. The shortage of unserviced land within ten miles of the city centre means that, in the current housing boom, Tibradden has a 'hope value' almost beyond measure. Its agricultural zoning would prove little deterrent to any interested developers, who would consider the six years until the next County Development Plan ample time to lobby councillors to have the land re-zoned. Our farm thus needs to be valued well in excess of the going agricultural rate.

I know the estate agent's assessment is correct. The developers' helicopters zigzag up and down the Kilmashogue valley several times a week, surveying our land. On the day of Charles's funeral, one of them buzzed around the Lawn and the Nineteen Acres for upwards of an hour. They have sent their heralds to our front door to make polite enquiries; some choose to inspect our house from the safety of their black Mercedes without getting out, and disappear back down the drive before I have a chance to stop them.

The most recent of these cold-called one dull afternoon, wishing to speak to the owner of the house on behalf of his client, a person, he said, with slow emphasis, of *very significant* means, who would be interested in purchasing the entire property. He introduced himself by handing me his business card from a well-known firm of solicitors. When I assured him I was as close to the owner as he was likely to get, he enquired whether I'd mind him asking how much land was with the house. Was it just the field in front of him, or was there more?

Yes, I replied, I did mind him asking. It took him a moment then to realize he was not going to be invited in. 'If you don't mind me asking you a question in return,' I continued lightly, 'did you see a for-sale sign at the bottom of our drive?' No, he did not. 'Well, if your house was for sale, would that not be your first step?' He smiled, a little more personably now to show he could appreciate a bit of repartee. Perhaps, he suggested apologetically, if he were to outline the sum his client had in mind? He was, he repeated, an individual of very considerable means . . . 'But I don't want to know how much my home is worth,' I told him, 'as it is not for sale.'

Nor indeed, I could have added, would it be mine to sell for quite some time. Paul, the trustee, had chuckled when I asked again recently how long the process of clearing probate and conveying the assets would take. 'Oh, anything between six months and several years. It depends on whether the Revenue accept our valuations. Even if they accept them initially, they can revisit them later, after your bill has been paid. You will just have to be patient.'

Patience is required with Susie, too. We are sitting in our usual places in the dining room, she in Charles's seat at the head of the table, I in the same chair I occupied as a child. Over the summer, the Friday meetings have stretched on occasion to more than an hour as I've tried to involve Susie in Teagasc's plans. For the most part, she has resisted their ideas strenuously. 'That REPS thing is a waste of time. The amount of work you need to do to keep them people happy. And there'll be fencing required. That'll cost money. Oh, yes, it's not worth the effort, I tell you, Miss Selina.'

In Susie's eyes, I am too inexperienced in agricultural matters to have any real authority. Book-learning is what my uncle and I have always been good at, a talent she respects right enough, but we will always need her to tell us how to run the land. I can cite the *Farmers Journal* all I like, but what I read one week is as likely, she tells me, to change the next. The department's officials are always chopping and changing the way they want things done on farms; the only sensible approach is to rely on personal experience of what has worked here in the past.

Two weeks ago, seventeen hoggets fetched €70 a head at Doyle's mart in Blessington, a price Joe said was 'about right'. I think it poor recompense for all the work he has put into them. The buckets of mineral lick for the ewes, which Susie wants me to order, cost €30 apiece. The wool cheque, for which the accountant had held out great hopes, amounted to €140 when it finally arrived, and that's before the €30 delivery fee is deducted. The vet's bill for testing cattle came to over €400 during the summer. Now Susie is telling me it has cost €888 to cut, bale and wrap the silage, and over €750 to reap and roll the oats, which were, she says, shot through with such quantities of barley, grass and weeds that we'd have been better off leaving it for the birds. That's despite paying our contractor over €1,000 to fertilize and spray the crop back in spring. Excluding wages, our farm expenditure over the five-month period since Charles died amounts to €5,060. Our farm income for the same period amounts to less than half this figure.

'Could we have done that?' I ask.

'What do you mean?' Susie replies sharply.

'Left the oats for the birds. Cut the field and then ploughed the stubble into the ground – would that have been a cheaper option?'

Susie gives me a thin smile. 'No. You couldn't do that, Miss Selina. The ground wouldn't be right for sowing after.'

I can see her summoning up all the necessary reserves of patience to deal with me. When I told her that I would be inheriting Tibradden, once all the legal work was through, she sagged visibly under the blow. I like to think this was less an expression of personal animosity than of disappointment that Master Niall would not succeed Master Charles as tradition would decree. The period of limbo, working on behalf of trustees she'd never met, had probably been as stressful for her as it had been for me. Master Niall's arrival as heir was something she had devoutly wished for as a deliverance from this uncertainty. I smiled and told her I thought that there were worse things than two women working together. At this she looked doubtful, but mustered a blessing: 'Well, I'm sure that you and Dr Graham will be very happy here, Miss Selina.'

Back in June, I asked Vincent and Seán whether they would talk Joe and Susie through the results of their farm inspection. I thought that Susie might accept the word of the Teagasc men more readily than mine; and I wanted Joe to be included in our discussions without incurring Susie's wrath for the breach of protocol that usually left her husband sitting outside in the car. Some sense of occasion was required, and it was managed. Joe, Susie and I sat round this same table together, and Vincent very carefully went through all the things he thought were being done right on the farm. The kind of respect he saw for nature in how the Kirwans currently farmed, he suggested, was at last being rewarded by schemes like REPS: Europe was beginning to value the old ways of doing things, to please the environmentalists. Some changes, of course, would have to be made, but many of these were about improving the look of things, removing sheep hurdles from fences and baths from fields, that kind of thing. Susie asked many questions, and each one was answered fully and considerately until she seemed satisfied. After they'd gone, she confided that she thought them 'a decent pair of gentlemen'. I, too, was impressed by the tact they'd shown.

We did not, however, touch on the need to sell the cattle. Vincent recommended I take the changes one step at a time: first establish the principle of entering REPS, then manage the consequences.

It is late October and I am sitting among thirty or so farmers in the Glenasmole Community Centre, waiting for Vincent and Seán to start tonight's lecture on nutrient management. I've come here straight from work. It is raining so hard outside that I had to pull over on the Featherbed and wait for it to ease off before I dared to creep down the boreen into the valley, grateful for the burned-out cars that marked off verge from bog. I have taken a chair next to the only other woman in the room; she introduces herself as Mary. The gas heaters fixed high on the wall give out a steady heat. Everyone else in the room seems to know one another. I peer at my toes, conscious of the squelch in my leather boots – I am the only person here who isn't wearing wellingtons.

It feels like some sort of achievement to be here at all. After five months of intense correspondence with the Department of Agriculture, I've begun to share Susie's scepticism about the worth of their bureaucracy. My queries about the fate of my application to the National Reserve Fund have been passed from my local inspector to the district office in Tallaght and on into the abyss that is the Single Farm Payment Section in Portlaoise. I keep a log of my calls until I reach the twenty-seventh, still unsure of the number of entitlements I might be allocated, their value, or when these issues will be resolved. I no longer regard the official view that my case is 'exceptional' as a compliment.

Over the next six weeks I immerse myself in the regulations that govern sustainable farming. I am the only beginner in the room. I try not to ask too many questions, but hover round

Mary in the tea-break, hoping she might tell me what 'pine-in-the-sheep' means, or 'braxy'.

The course gives me the chance to view Tibradden's farming woes within a wider context. Under REPS, we are told, stocking densities are kept low, down to one cow or – marvellously – 6.66 sheep per hectare. This is more than twice the density of sheep grazing Tibradden at present. Spreading lime lowers the soil's acidity, helping grass to absorb nitrogen and reducing the amount of fertilizer used. This is why our neighbours' fields up the mountain are greener than our own. At least two out of a list of fourteen measures must be undertaken within the first two years: these include the planting of broadleaf trees in open fields, the maintenance and repair of dry-stone walls, allowing public access to archaeological sites and the creation of new wildlife habitats. Supplementary payments can be earned through the establishment of native apple orchards and – most lucratively of all, at a maximum of €1,300 for 2.5 hectares – the sowing of bird-seed. This brings to mind what Susie said about our poor crop of winter oats in the Eleven Acres. The scale of payments is designed to make REPS attractive to farmers on small-holdings, engaged in part-time non-dairy livestock enterprises, like our own, for which market prices barely meet the cost of production, not the beef barons of Meath or the dairy kings of north Cork. By the end of the year, it is expected that 50,000 Irish farms will be in REPS, with holdings averaging 30 hectares and an average REPS payment of €7,000. Although all farm payments are conditional on their recipients continuing to engage in 'agricultural activities', this no longer necessarily means rearing livestock or growing crops: 'activity' is defined simply as 'maintaining the land in good agricultural order'. Stripped of their fragrant environmentalism, the real intention behind these measures is to take marginal land out of agricultural production, consigning it to forestry or nature, while allowing the full-scale commercialization of European agriculture to continue apace elsewhere.

The list of tasks and regulations is very long. Farm buildings must be painted in the vernacular colours authorized by the Department of Agriculture (rust red, dark green and grey), and screened from the surrounding countryside by stands of trees, with native oak, whitebeam and ash preferred to the planters' beeches that glow along the avenues of big country houses. This has nothing to do with nationalist sentiment: where a whitebeam might support 5,000 species of flora and fauna, a beech is considered barren with a mere 500. Extra subsidies are provided for keeping pedigree breeding stock of our native species, including Kerry cattle, Connemara ponies and Galway sheep. ('Don't be tempted,' warns a classmate, when I enquire about the latter. 'When those animals roll over they can't right themselves, they're that heavy. They die with their four feet stuck up in the air.') There is special provision, too, for harvesting hay meadows from the centre out in the Shannon callows, to reduce the likelihood of catching corncrakes in the threshing blades. My great-grandfather, the Colonel, shot what was probably the last corncrake seen on Glendhu Mountain in 1936. In the break, a farmer from Glencullen tells me his father used to beat for the Colonel, alongside other neighbours from the valley, on the big annual shooting parties.

Of the thirty or so in my class, at least half are in their fifties, some older, including one man who looks to be Susie's age. His white hair is stained nicotine yellow; his sheepskin jacket belongs to a more substantial frame. They are mostly sheep farmers, whose animals graze the commonage on top of Glendhu and Kippure. The majority also keep small herds of suckler cattle they raise in the lower fields around Bohernabreena reservoir. Commonage rights, passed down through families, are measured here in callops – a callop being the amount of land it takes to graze the animal most usually stocked on any particular stretch of commonage, whether it be sheep, cow, horse or goat. Later Vincent will tell me that in the townland of Castlekelly, at the Kippure end of the Glenasmole valley, the callop needed to graze an upland ewe translates into 1.039 hectares of heath. This year, when for the first time the payment a farmer receives from Brussels no longer takes account of what is produced on the farm, this unit of measurement, based on an intimate knowledge of the land and what it can support, has finally become obsolete.

When I ask Vincent how older farmers, like the gentleman in the sheepskin coat, have fared in complying with the new regulations, he shakes his head sadly before explaining that in places where verbal agreements between one generation and the next have tended to stand in lieu of wills, it has been hard to find evidence supporting the hill-farmers' claims to any given number of callops. In the transition from headage payments to area-based schemes, farmers who cannot document their land holdings, most often the poorest, are losing out the most.

Under REPS, the number of livestock allowed on commonage is to be reduced. In theory, this is to allow the heather and fraughan bushes to reclaim the mountain-tops. 'Not that that's bloody likely round here,' one man grumbles to the room. Hill-walkers and dogs stamp more tracks across the Featherbed than the sheep ever have. 'Sure some Sundays you'd be out and there'd be cars all along the top road, and the dogs are just let off the leash with no regard for ewes about to yean or anything. And then there are the kids on scrambling bikes . . .' After we've finished, I commiserate with him about it all – the noisy encroachment of a city in search of peace and quiet in a landscape considered empty – but realize, too, that the proximity of urban jobs is what has kept these valleys populated and halfway prosperous. There isn't a full-time farmer in the room,

Mary assures me: 'I mean no one could be now, with the way it's going, not on this scale, not up here.'

On the way home across the Featherbed that first night, I passed a burning car, still blazing on the roadside despite the rain. Further on, three cars packed with teenagers were parked facing the glen, headlights on, wipers going, little to see bar the wet and the bog and the blurred lights of Tallaght beyond. Up above, the transmission mast on Kippure flashed its new white warning lights onto the low cloud. I thought about how my account of the evening would have amused Charles; how he would have set down the crossword and got up from his chair in the drawing room to hunt out a photograph of a shooting party at Cruagh and read out the names of the participants penned in on the back, looking for the name of my classmate's father among the beaters. Or he might have searched out the Colonel's game diaries and found with a gleeful giggle the few days when the tallies of snipe, widgeon, woodcock and grouse shot by Father Behan and the gamekeeper, Stubbs, outnumbered his own grandfather's poorer bag. But Charles's greatest amusement, masking a supportive concern, would have been reserved for the efforts I was making now, returning home at ten thirty on a Tuesday night after a day's lecturing, to have a semi-feudal and long-neglected estate recognized as the very latest in EU-subsidized, environmentally sustainable agriculture.

Down in the yard, the new ram looks like Tony Soprano, which Colin and I think is a good thing, but he also reminds me of the model sheep/footstool they used to have in Bunratty Woollen Mills, which might be bad. We bought a Texel because the flock, according to Joe, was 'getting too pure-bred'. Hybridity, apparently, guarantees hardiness, particularly of the hoofs. 'Let's hope there's a bit of spring in him,' Joe says, punching a tag through the ram's left ear. At €500 hammer price at Doyle's, he had better be well sprung. We have already enjoyed a confusing conversation, over breakfast, about his possible prowess, with Joe announcing that of all the rams on show he'd picked the best: 'Some of them had no length in them at all, they need a bit of length, but your fella would be a good two foot or so long, so he should be fine.' I can't help thinking that this pedigree specimen is wasted on our lame and ragged ewes, but without a ram there'll be no lambs in spring.

The purchase of the ram is also an attempt to boost Joe's morale. I recently told him that the cattle would have to be sold before Christmas. He took the news quietly, but I saw that it hurt. I knew he'd particularly regret letting go the heifer calf, an Aberdeen Angus cross that had been born the same week that Charles died. He could understand why I had to do it, he told me then, but he'd prefer not to load them up himself. He'd ask Susie to call John Murphy and see if he would bring the bullocks to the Kepak meat factory, and the heifers to Doyle's.

In the interstices of the day, as the sparrowhawk flies from the lime across the old tennis court, the Lawn begins to resonate differently. What I had thought of as natural is, I now understand, a landscape designed by successive owners and engineered by hired hands. During the break at our REPS lecture on soils and drainage, another farmer explained to me what lies beneath the green pastures of farms like ours: a series of little stone channels of about a foot's width, laid at five-foot intervals in a gravel bed to drain surface water away into the perimeter ditches. 'If you cut back the brambles and clear the sides you should be able to see thin streams trickling out in a storm,' he told me. The land he used to rent for grazing at Stocking Lane, sold last year for a housing estate of 1,500 units, is now flooded, because 'they've broken up the old drains and have yet to lay the new'.

I think about the men who dug the gullies and laid the stones to create the drains, how the gravel would have been dug from the river bed, fetched by donkey and cart up the slope, piled out, pitched in, then the earth packed back on top, over and over again. I wonder what they were paid. I don't know whether this work was carried out for John Jones, whose house at Tibradden, described in 1839 as being of 'tolerably good repair', provided the foundations for Mary Davis's new residence when she married Thomas Hosea Guinness. Perhaps the heavy labour was undertaken earlier by John Murphy, named in an indenture of 1736 as the tenant here of Speaker Connolly under a fee-farm grant. The marriage of his daughter, Bridget, to Jeffrey Davis first brought these lands into the Davis family. Maybe it was earlier still, on the orders of Peter Talbot de Bulloch, into whose hands much of the townland passed during the reign of King Henry VIII when it was confiscated from its previous owners, the Fitzgeralds, on their conviction for high treason. But if it was worth confiscating, most likely the fields had already been drained for the Kilmainham Priory of St John at Jerusalem, which held the lands from the late 1100s.

When the first mistress of Tibradden, Mary Guinness (*née* Davis), was a child, she would have watched workers pass through this field on their way to the mills powered by the River Glin. The women walking down to work in Mr Hughes's silk factory and Mr Doolan's flour mill would have made use of the old drive that is now the gentle hollow I used to trace home from school. In the 1840s there were thirteen mills on the River Owendoher and the River Glin, employing between twenty and 120 people each, making paper, silk, wool and flour. One, run by Moses Verney in the 1760s, made paper foil to prevent gold and silver lace from tarnishing, used in the main, I fancy, for keeping ecclesiastical fineries bright at the altar. There might even have been a small domestic market for Mr Verney's product within Whitechurch parish, for the parish was prosperous. The 1841 census records that only 2.9 per cent of its population lived in 'category one' housing (one-room cabins), compared with 28.8 per cent for County Dublin as a whole; and the number of good farm- and town-houses was nearly twice the county average. Despite this prosperity, the same source reveals that over the four years to 1841 the parish population dropped by a fifth to 2,354 inhabitants. A cholera cess of a penny an acre levied by the parish in the early 1830s, to fund the whitewashing of buildings, suggests an outbreak that may account for the early deaths of Mary's brothers and mother.

When Mary was growing up, the view from Tibradden would have been crowded and busy with carts and people in the foreground. But by the early 1860s, when her husband, Thomas Hosea Guinness, decided to put in a boating pond on the River Glin and plant its banks with Noble fir, Spanish chestnut and cherry laurel, the mills and laundries had gone and the unlit city must have seemed to loom closer as the fields and river emptied of industry. The estate became one of the main local employers: labourers, beaters, gardeners, a gamekeeper, men to clear the silt from the traps in the river and to maintain the boat-ponds.

In his plans for the estate, Thomas Hosea was doing no more than following the fashion of his class and time. Almost four per cent of the total landed area of Ireland was given over to demesne parks by the mid-nineteenth century. Tracts of forested rides, deer parks and shrubberies attest to the craze for picturesque landscapes where one might safely take a turn in the evening air, or exercise while enjoying the vagaries of a carefully cultivated nature. Pheasants scooting out from the rhododendrons, herons picking their way through the ripple of their own reflections, hares chasing each other through the long grasses – these were the daily pleasures gentlemen recorded in the field notes that intersperse their diaries. Here and elsewhere, demesne land was lost to productive farming, despite the herds of ornamental cattle lumbering through the buttercups. The well-stocked pond-walks along the stream resounded to the noise of guns and field-dogs, providing game for the table and sport for guests.

It is nearing Christmas. The lack of central heating causes us to huddle around the fire in our bedroom most evenings. I find myself leaning forward, staring into the flames as my grandmother once did. There are no answers here to the questions that nag at my conscience. I've learned all I can from the REPS course, I have my certificate, and when the land is transferred into my name I can draw up the contract and wait to draw down the cheque. What bothers me are the larger implications of the course's easy slogans: 'Less is more'; 'Don't farm for the sake of it'. Joe's life challenge has been to produce some marketable commodity from his given acres. He has fixed fences and mended gaps in hedges for the sole purpose of keeping livestock in or out, because livestock have value and to lose a beast means you are out of pocket. And of course you care for the animals you have raised and tended and spent your paid and unpaid hours looking after. What does it do to Joe to see me sell the few cattle he's raised so that I can fill in a form proving I've taken steps to keep the water clean? What does it mean to take a field like the Seven Acres that used to yield a barley crop and sow it with a mixture of kale and linseed to encourage yellowhammers to feed on it in the winter?

10.

Through wintertime we call on spring,
And through the spring on summer call,
And when abounding hedges ring
Declare that winter's best of all.
W. B. Yeats, 'The Wheel'

March 2005

Two foxes lie under the lime tree in the warm sun. The wheel
has turned again. The bare snow that made the roads around
Glencullen and the Sally Gap treacherous has melted quickly
away. A doe and her fawn are tiptoeing very cautiously under
the sweet chestnut tree towards the tulips budding in the garden, where they will feast again as they did yesterday. The ewes
are due to lamb any day now.

This morning Major McDowell phoned to discuss the fence
across Marymount. When he purchased St Thomas from my
uncle in 1976, he persuaded Charles to sell a further thirty acres
on the opposite side of the stream. The bargain they struck
then has seen us renting back the Eleven Acres for our unprofitable crop of winter oats ever since. In addition, we have been
paying the Major an annual fee for grazing the bottom section
of Marymount in the absence of any fence to separate his land
from ours. Before Christmas, I informed the Major that we
would not be renewing these annual agreements when they
were up at the end of the year. I would take our animals off the

field, and we could discuss erecting a fence there in the spring. He expressed no surprise at my decision. Instead, he quizzed me gently about how I intended to farm Tibradden. He was in no particular hurry, he said then, to clear our sheep off his pasture if I needed time to establish these plans.

Yesterday's conversation changes things. I may not be aware, he suggested, that the 1976 deed of sale contained a clause committing the vendor to erect a boundary at his own expense to the purchaser's satisfaction. When the land is conveyed to me, I will also inherit the responsibility to fulfil this outstanding condition of the sale. While it mattered little to him at this stage in his life whether he lived to see the fence erected or not, he felt obliged to tell me that a property developer had recently approached him about buying his lands for a golf course. If he were to sell – and he stressed the real negotiations had yet to begin – he feared this new owner might exact a more expensive boundary treatment than the standard sheep fence that would do for him. It would be in my best interests, he thought, to honour this outstanding condition sooner rather than later. 'Yes, I understand,' I told him, still trying to absorb all the implications.

The Major sounded embarrassed when he next spoke: 'I think these people are interested in talking to any neighbours who might be prepared to sell them more land. If it suited, I could send them on up to you.'

Towards the end of March, the trustees call me in to sign the deed of appointment conveying Charles's land and livestock to me. The house and one acre will follow under a separate deed of conveyance some time later. I sign my name at the place indicated and feel, with both men standing by, that I am releasing myself from a prolonged period of adolescence.

Travelling back on the Luas, I think about all the other places

I once imagined living my life. In my early twenties, I spent a year in London coasting on the adrenalin rush of the city while trying to work out what buoy might keep me afloat. Before that, living in Budapest, for the first time fully alone, I remember leaning out over the rail of Erzsébet Bridge at dawn to watch a seagull cruising on the wind that always blew along the Danube and realizing some moments later that, far, far from the sea, I was nonetheless searching for a tidal mark along the quays.

The horizon Tibradden then cast on the future had appeared distantly, like the momentary glimpse of water through trees, a destination I'd arrive at sooner or later. In my mind's eye, it never changed. I used to fear that once I arrived, the horizon would recede further and I would stand on the front steps marooned in the past, mesmerized by my family's history shimmering in its dying arc.

But I've begun to question recently whether this elegiac note always has to drown other tunes in places like this. However much it means to me, in the end Tibradden is just a house and some fields, a property to be farmed and worked at and lived in untidily. Tramping through the field across the river, the solicitor's map once more in hand, I realize I no longer think of this field as Marymount, but have slipped into Susie's ways and name it first the Nineteen Acres. My eye for the landscape, too, has changed. Since the REPS course, I notice the grass not as a background wash or colour, but as a crop. Tasks now attach to these acres: I must find out the costs of spreading lime, and fertilizer, and talk to Susie about getting the pasture harrowed to maximize the growth in this good weather.

The children came at Christmas, shivered over hot-water bottles in the absence of central heating, and went home again. In January their mother rang to say that Mel, Colin's youngest daughter, wanted to come and live with us. We agreed that if by Easter she still wished to move, we would try to find a place in the local school for September. It now looks certain she will come. The old ties, dressing-gowns, stamp collections and paperbacks that were pushed to one side in the wardrobe to make room for my shirts will have to be cleared out for my stepdaughter. At eleven, she will be exactly the same age I was when I first came to live here.

There is a certain poetic justice in her decision. I remember putting her to bed one night in the spare bedroom, about five years ago, when she asked me, 'What is Charles's real name?' The question bamboozled me; all the answers I suggested were rejected firmly one by one.

It was her daddy who understood, asking gently, 'Do you mean "Uncle"?' Yes, that was it, she said.

'You can call him that too, if you like,' I told her, but she never took up the offer. To call Charles 'Uncle' would have been a step too far, then, in the tricky conduct of her relations with me and my family. Now she would come, and it would be my turn to provide the care and security which my grandmother had provided me: routine, care, stability, and the best of love I can manage.

In April, I discover an ordinary miracle has occurred. I am pregnant. All being well, the baby is due in early December. Food, sleep, heat, power are all that seem to matter now. The trustees struggle to appreciate how urgent the house repairs have just become. The house can be conveyed to me only when the Revenue accepts the trustees' assessment of the amount of tax due on the estate. When this is paid, and the property is in my name, we can approach the bank for a mortgage to fund all the necessary work. Until I am the legal owner, the solicitor emphasizes when I press the matter again, I should not undertake any more than the bare essentials of home maintenance, financed, if required, by a personal loan. I try to explain that with my stepdaughter due to arrive in the autumn, and a baby due in winter, it simply isn't feasible to wait any longer for heat and safe electricity. Eventually they concede that the ordinary demands of living cannot reasonably be suspended until my trusteeship comes to an end. I return home and make an appointment with the bank to arrange a bridging loan, then call up our plumbers and electrician to book them in for the summer.

In May, I receive a phone call from Oliver Schurmann. Our wedding guests bought us vouchers for his perennials nursery in Stocking Lane, less than a mile away. On one of my shopping trips there, I mentioned our walled garden. He would like, he says now, to come over and take a look at it, as he is seeking a suitable place to relocate his nursery.

He arrives in the middle of a downpour. The rain doesn't dampen his enthusiasm in the least, even as I open the garden door onto the dark green thatch of Queen Anne's lace and hogweed, flowering white and cream in the full flush of early summer. He pushes them aside and strides ahead of me to the vegetable patch we've cleared, where he bends down and scoops up a handful of black soil. I can see its quality pleases him. The weeds I despaired of clearing – bindweed, ground elder, creeping buttercup, celandines – are thriving on the heritage of Paddy Flanagan's labour. Wheelbarrows of potash from the ashpit in the courtyard, compost, manure, fine sand and river gravel, the straw dug in after the strawberries were finished: the record of his hours of digging is still present in the nurturing loam.

Oliver asks me about the apple trees: why do their branches grope like fingers towards the light? I explain how little I know of pruning fruit trees, and he says he likes the way they've grown wild and untrained, as if they're in the Burren. I could, I tell him, still plant the four quarters of this garden from memory: the helianthus with the butterflies, the clump of hostas under the old pear tree, the rosemary for remembrance by my grandmother's seat, bachelor's buttons in the annual beds along the wall. But I lack the time to tend it, and I'd rather see it used by others than let the jungle win. 'Yes,' he says abstractedly. He likes to paraglide, and he is surveying the surrounding greenery the way he would if, instead of standing here, he were gauging the distance to the ground below before jumping off a cliff. He will have to confer with Liat, his wife and business partner, and I will have to talk to the trustees, but I see the idea has taken root. With any luck, Mount Venus Nursery will become our tenants at Tibradden.

In August, Colin hires a van and goes to fetch Mel and her pet rabbit from Hull. Together we unpack her clothes into the same drawers and wardrobe I once used. When Peter has finished installing the new sockets and switches, we will replace the old wallpaper, with its posies and curling ribbons, with something plainer that she can decorate with her own posters and photographs of her siblings. So long as we can observe the daily rhythms familiar from the many holidays she has spent here with Jo and Seamus, we can keep her loneliness at bay. But with the start of school, and the commencement of our own terms, we are both concerned she will feel the loss more fully. It will be hard to be the new girl in a sixth class that has been together since junior infants.

On the last day of the summer holidays, Colin and I take her down to pick crab apples from the Lower Lawn just as my grandmother used to do with me. Her father scythes away the nettles before we take up sticks to knock the fruit down from the highest branches as Mel tries gleefully to catch the sour apples in her bucket. Walking back, all three together, the bucket full for crab apple jelly, I wonder if she, too, will find a refuge in this pastoral setting where the complexities of her family can be thought through and accepted, if never wholly resolved.

By the time we all start back at school, the whole house is spilling its guts in wires and pipes and displaced floorboards. Seán and Barry, our plumbers, bore a three-inch hole through the wall with a carborundum drill and afterwards present me with a foot-long granite cylinder to use for a rolling pin. When I can, I retreat into our bedroom, put in earplugs, try to stop my mind manically preparing lists and instead catch up on the sleep I've been deprived of by my kicking baby.

In mid-October, the solicitor calls me in to sign the documents conveying the house to me. All bills and outstanding debts have been met by the sale of Charles's shares, which he'd inherited from his father. Roger, the accountant, tells me that my uncle always knew this cushion would be needed, and that this is one reason he was reluctant to sell the shares even when short of cash. I try to keep up with all the figures the trustees are presenting, but realize shamefully that I am going to cry. I concentrate on the nondescript print on the wall opposite, but memories of Charles's death and residual worries about our future, the baby and Mel refuse to be quieted by the corporate hush of the office. The trustees are kind and understanding but surely regret the glass walls of our meeting room as I try to turn my head away to hide from the curious stares of passers-by.

I stop work at Hallowe'en. By late November, my feet have swollen to twice their normal size. On the midwife's instructions, I spend the evenings bouncing on a colossal pink ball, like Violet Beauregarde inflated astride her bubble-gum. Mel has been keeping me plied with cup after cup of raspberry-leaf tea ever since I told her its purpose in triggering labour. She, too, is excited now. Peter, Seán and Barry are all still here, working faster since we started enquiring about their obstetric skills.

Punctually on his due date, the third of December, our first son, Kim, is born, weighing eight pounds and six ounces, with jet-black hair. My mind struggles to catch up with my body's achievement. He is impossibly real, at last not of me but of himself. When we are left alone in the delivery room, all three, a calm joy descends amid the mess of birth. Later that night, Colin drives us home from Holles Street. He cranes around at each traffic light to check that Kim is still with us. And he is: a tiny body marooned in the car-seat, his marsupial eyes astonished by the world, by its distances and rush, the interplay of shadows on the retina. When we open the front door, we turn on a new light in the hall and find a note from Peter, telling us that he has finished rewiring the house over the thirty-six hours I've been in labour. Light and heat, food and rest, love and gratitude are all that matter now.

II.

January 2006

I am in Mel's room, struggling to persuade her that her shorter haircut looks great and there's no need to plaster it down with so much mousse. We had been getting on fine until a trip to the hairdresser in late November. Now when she looks in the mirror all she sees is the distance from her mother, brother and sister in Hull. The girl who looks back at her is someone she is not yet ready to become. Right now, though, she needs to get ready for school or we will be late.

The sudden sound of a car pulling up outside the window interrupts our discussion. I look out. J.J. Doherty, a friend of Joe's who breeds and shoots pheasants in the set-aside fields beyond, casts a glance up as he opens the door. He looks stricken. Colin gets to the door ahead of me as the doorbell sounds; his voice is urgent, loud. 'Quick,' he says, as I pick up Kim from Mel's bed and rush downstairs, 'J.J. thinks Joe has hung himself.'

I pass the baby to Colin and run down the drive with J.J. 'I think he's in the tractor shed,' he says, as we turn the corner. Beyond the cedars, there is a weight in the dark rectangle of the shed. 'Oh, God, don't look,' says J.J., but we rush forward anyway. It is Joe, his body is hanging in the entrance. His black woollen hat is still on, gumboots, and his coat. His cold, cold face is slumped to the right, his eyes shut. I see his swollen mouth, then the weal at his neck from the rope he secured to one of the supporting beams. His skin has purpled into a crust along the edge, like the swelling of bark around barbed wire. The ladder he used to climb up stands upright against the tin wall. I have to raise my head to look at him, as I have never had to before. He looks too meagre and vulnerable to have done this violence to himself. It seems grotesque to stand here within touching distance and say nothing to him, nothing but the chorus of 'You poor, poor man' that runs away with my tongue.

We are intruding on his privacy. I feel I have no right to trespass so intimately. We look towards the lodge. A light is on in the main room. I reach towards Joe's body, wanting to get him down, laid out, confer some dignity, before Susie appears, but J.J. stops me. 'We'll have to wait for the guards,' he says. Susie rang him earlier this morning when she discovered Joe had gone from the house, and asked J.J. to look for him when he didn't return. He'd been on his way up to ask our help when he saw the shadow in the shed.

'I'll have to tell her,' I say, 'before she comes out.'

Susie does not look up when I push open the door and call her name. Her fingers continue to trace patterns in the crumbs on the table. Joseph must still be in bed. I can see she fears the worst. I take her hands in mine. The palms are smooth and white and soft. I tell her as best I can. She starts to weep quietly and we sit together for a time, before she asks me, in sheer bewilderment, 'What will come of us now?' I hear the noise of sirens. Then the sound of neighbours arriving; all were told by the postman, who stands there with J.J., visibly shaken by the scene.

Colin is outside. He has laid a coat out on the ground beneath the cedars, and Joe's body is lying on it, the rope trailing out from the cloth over his head. Jeeps and Land Rovers, Garda cars, a fire engine and an ambulance are thrown up on the verge, and the men congregate to one side, absorbing the shock. A Ban Garda takes me aside to ask me questions I find myself unable to answer. I can feel my milk coming in for Kim's morning feed. I leave Susie in the good care of neighbours, promising to return later with dinner for her and Joseph.

They had been due to meet me at ten this morning. On Christmas Day, when I called in with presents to the lodge, Susie had started to ask me about Joe's pension and I'd stopped her, telling her I would discuss it with them in the New Year as promised. Last night I sat down and prepared all the figures, ready to show Susie how if Joe, who had just turned seventy-seven, finally claimed the state pension he'd been entitled to since turning sixty-five, and I topped up this amount with two-thirds of his current wages for half the number of days, they would all be much better off. I could assure Susie that there was no condition attached to the state pension that would prevent Joe from continuing to receive an income from any source. From my point of view, the third I saved in the wage bill could be used to hire in someone else to handle the heavier work as required. Now, it seems clear that Joe's worries were of a different order completely, and my belief that I could address them through such arrangements seems naïve.

In late summer, Joe had slipped and injured his leg while up fixing the water supply in Larch Hill. He had required an operation on his knee followed by a period of recuperation at St James's Hospital. One day I went in to visit him and found him gone – he'd discharged himself early. All who knew him had recognized that trying to keep him inside, with his leg up, would be an impossible task. Shortly after he left hospital I'd seen him limping through the long grasses with the dogs, stopping for a rest only after he'd cast a covert glance towards the house to check no one was watching. Until the accident, he was still shearing sheep, vigorous work for any man and some indication of his exceptional strength, despite the small build that had earned him the local nickname of 'the dote Kirwan'. He knew, and I knew, and Susie knew that after the accident some of the farm work was beyond what his body would allow.

Some time back in the autumn I'd proposed to Joe that we reduce the flock. He could continue to do as much as he felt able for, and I would bring in someone else to work alongside him, someone he liked whom, I suggested, he might train in. I was anxious lest he feel pushed out, and I had learned from our Friday conversations that the prospect of someone else farming the land he and Susie considered their own territory was a source of dread. However, in the past few years, Joe had made a good friend, named John, who was willing to help out whenever he could now that he was retired. I got the impression that John, and another neighbour, had been called on more and more over the past year, but as far as possible the Kirwans had kept their comings and goings quiet. They did not want to be seen as dependent on others to continue in their work. While I understood this well, the trustees had warned me about employer's and public liability in the event of any accident, and it seemed to me only fair that anyone putting in hours on the farm should be paid for their work.

Whenever I spoke of these concerns to Susie, she dismissed them as if I'd insulted her. Sure it was a pleasure to a man who lived down in the city to be up here in the fresh air, she said, and he wasn't looking for money. It was good for him to be taking the exercise. Besides, if anything were to happen to him on the farm he wasn't one of those people who would take me to court. I didn't doubt any of this, but the situation made me uncomfortable and I resolved to speak directly to John. Eventually, he agreed under protest to accept a token cheque for any days he helped out with heavier tasks.

In the run-up to Christmas, Joe had called into the kitchen

with a letter from the pensions board. He wanted me to explain it to him, he said. In truth, this meant reading it aloud. He had called at a bad time. I was trying to prepare dinner for my mother-in-law, Dorothy, who was visiting for a few days, and Kim, still only a fortnight old, needed to be changed. Instead of bringing Joe upstairs to the privacy of the dining room, I had gone through the letter with him then and there, knowing that Dorothy's full attention would be absorbed by her new grandson.

The letter said a cheque would issue shortly for a sum amounting to almost two years' wages in back-payments. He received the information without enthusiasm. I found this difficult to understand. I thought he might not have grasped the figure fully, or that he feared in some way it was undeserved. I repeated that this bonanza was money he had earned through the social insurance stamps paid out of his wages by Charles. In essence, all he was doing now was reclaiming the pot of savings long ago set aside for his use.

He seemed incapable of absorbing this. Conscious of my mother-in-law standing by, and the baby needing my attention, I didn't probe further into what was worrying him. Instead I arranged to go through it all properly on the first Friday in January, when I'd ask Colin to mind Kim. Joe lingered for a minute then, as if he were finding something else to say, but in the end he just picked up his cap and walked out the kitchen door. If I had only shown him more courtesy, paid more attention to the fact that Joe did not share my delight at the money announced in the letter, he might have confided in me then.

The last time Joe and I had had a proper conversation had been on St Stephen's Day. Before Christmas I'd invited him in for dinner. 'Ah, no thanks, Selina,' he'd replied. 'I can't settle in a house for too long, I start to get a bit restless, if it's all the same to you.'

'Well, come in then for some stout and Christmas cake,' I'd pressed. 'I'd like you to meet the baby.'

He stayed for just short of an hour. We never usually ran out of things to say. After local news, there would be stories from when he had worked in the forestry, or, if these failed, I could ask him for stories about the other families who had worked here over the years: the Farrells, Flanagans, Nolans, Stubbses, Wisdoms, Plants and Valentines. He didn't want to hold Kim, saying he was afraid he'd still have the yard-dirt on him, although he'd put on his good clothes and was as spruced up as he'd been for our wedding. So I insisted and laid the baby gently in his arms. We saw then that something was wrong, because he kept his eyes low and avoided looking at Kim's wide-awake and quiet face, and I knew he was a soft man who would normally be delighted, as he had been when I'd told him I was expecting.

'What's wrong, Joe?' I asked, relieving him of Kim.

He replied unexpectedly that a *Prime Time* special he'd seen about drink-driving had been playing on his mind. He'd given up going to Doherty's for his customary pint of Bass on a Friday night since the new limit came in. He'd heard the guard tell the interviewer that anyone taken in for breathalysing would be locked in a police cell while the paperwork was attended to, and it had stayed with him. 'I wouldn't like that, you know, to hear the door close in on me. To hear that door slam: I don't think I could survive it.' He had his cap in his hands and he sat looking down at it while his fingers worked their way round and round its brim.

'But, Joe,' I protested, 'Colin or I could easily arrange to come and collect you from the pub. Sure it's only down the road.' No, he said, he wouldn't put us to the trouble. Anyway, with the medication he was taking for his knee, the doctor said you weren't meant to have alcohol. His glass, I noticed then, was still half full.

I put his new teetotalism down to Susie. I'd heard that she'd given her husband a terrible earful when he came home in a drunken state after an autumn sale at Blessington mart. As far as I could tell, Joe's two escapes from the bleak confines of the lodge were the fields and Doherty's on Friday night in the company of the farming men he'd grown up with on the slopes beneath the Hell Fire Club.

I could add to this now the Sunday mass in Ballyroan. Until the priest arrived today, I hadn't known Joe to be a practising Catholic.

When I return to the lodge before dinner, Anne-Marie, our nearest neighbour, opens the door. She and her family have drawn up a rota to sit with Susie and Joseph over the next few days. Sam, her husband, will sleep tonight in the Jeep parked immediately outside. She has stew prepared and has brought over an electric slow-cooker so that Susie can reheat the dinners that are left in to her. She's had sweet tea, and bread and butter, but won't take anything else. If I don't mind, she'll take the chance now to get the dinner on in her own house. She'll pop in again later.

Someone has lit the fire. Joseph is sitting in a chair beside it, rocking backwards and forwards as he usually does, his dark head bent over the blue baler twine he works incessantly through his fingers. 'Does he know?' I ask Susie quietly, after a while.

'Ah, no,' she says. 'How could he understand, when I don't understand it myself?'

The small room is fuggy with the smell of stale cooking, animals and smoke. The evidence of mice is everywhere. It is quiet without the television on, just the squeak of the leatherette as Joseph rocks to and fro. Again Susie asks me what will become of them. 'You'll be all right, Susie,' I say gently, but in her grief and fear she won't let the matter go.

One day last autumn I met Joe on the corner of the drive. The day was bright and breezy, an optimistic warmth presaging the harvest. I asked him about Cruagh, how his own lambs were coming on over there. He'd answered me with the non-sequitur that he'd sworn, when his mother left him the place, never to sell it. I was taken aback. 'Why, has someone made you an offer?' I asked. Nothing like that at all, it appeared. He was uncharacteristically downcast. 'What's worrying you?' I finally asked.

He said nothing for a moment, before quietly asking, with his head turned away from me, 'How's it all going to end?' This was around the time I had first broached the idea of bringing in help for the farm work, so I answered him as if he were speaking of retirement. But in truth, he meant more than that and I sensed it and shied away from facing it.

Joseph was at the heart of his fears. Confined to the car or lodge by his mother, who trusted no one else to care for him, he was too strong for his parents to look after him indefinitely into their old age. A woman whose mother had worked at Tibradden once told me in the supermarket how Kitty had taught Joseph to walk, taking him out to the tennis court daily, and, later, how to kick a ball around. My own mother, she said, had pressed Susie to allow Joseph to attend a school for children with intellectual disabilities, but whenever he caught a cold he was pulled out of education. Now the only one allowed to visit was the public health nurse, who came once a week to attend to both Susie and Joseph, bringing with her the necessary provisions for Joseph's special diet. 'Nothing there will change,' the woman in the supermarket told me, 'until Susie accepts a degree of change herself.'

Joe had been trying to work out the puzzle of their lives for himself. When I had enquired at Christmas, he said he was not sleeping well. He didn't like to take the tablets the doctor had given him because they gave him nightmares. He preferred to get up and make himself busy. He didn't like watching television at that hour, and he wouldn't want the sound to wake up Susie. Accustomed as she was to his departure from the bed beside her in the early hours, she had not got up this morning when she heard the soft sound of the lock being turned and Joe letting himself out. When he did not return for his breakfast, her first thought must have been that he had fallen again while out on his rounds, and that was why she called J.J. to look first in the yard, and then at the water supply in Larch Hill. But I sensed, when I told her the news, that the part of her that had always feared the worst was not surprised.

'Joe, do you have a bit of twine? More twine, Joe.'

Joseph's voice rings out in perfect mimicry of his mother, his habitual chorus now twisted horribly by his father's death into an unconscious taunt. Spools of twine lie at his feet, the lengths Joe must have cut for him yesterday before he searched out the length of rope for himself. 'A farmer's best friend,' he used to call it, unravelling the blue lines in his pocket to tie up fence or gate.

'Where is the roll, Susie?' I ask, knowing that Joseph will keep up his chorus until someone goes to fetch him more, as his father did about this time every evening when he came in from the fields.

'Ah, don't mind him, Miss Selina,' she says, even now guarding the door to the bedroom where it is kept. 'He'll settle down in a minute.'

But Joseph will not be quieted. 'Do you have a bit of twine, Joe?' he continues to sing out, pushing away the lengths I pass him. Long minutes pass as his chant goes on.

'Jesus, Joseph, would you ever stop?' cries Susie suddenly, her voice breaking for the first time, her shoulders heaving in deep shudders of grief.

I pick up the bread knife from the table and go in search of what he wants. An electric-blue bundle is visible stuffed in beside the boiler. Joseph takes the new length in his fingers and sniffs it curiously before rubbing it against his cheek. I put my hand on his shiny black hair and leave it there for a moment, useless and disregarded. He and I are the same age. I cannot think what I might do for him now.

I can bring in meals, I can make arrangements, I can sit and hold their hands. But I realize, as the time passes, that my presence affords Susie very little comfort. Since Charles died, I have represented the hard thought of tomorrow from which there is no rest. 'I am so sorry,' I tell her finally, releasing her and rising from the table. 'I am so sorry I did not do more.'

'Sure what could you have done, Miss Selina? Or any of us?' Her voice has no sharpness to it, but is just plain and heavy. 'Why he did it I'll never know.'

That night, as I lie awake, Joe's body hangs behind my eyes: a stilled pendulum in the dark. Beside me, my baby lies ticking 'like a fat gold watch'. How do you knot a noose, I find myself wondering, resisting the pull towards Kim's warmth. The knot is vivid in the morning light, and despite myself I begin to count its loops as one otherwise might count the rungs of a ladder, up towards the top rung and the step into the dark, the moment of flight: the crumpled shock into which is poured the figure of Joe whom I, so carelessly and irrelevantly, loved.

In the days that follow, I learn that Joe sold his own sheep back in November at Blessington mart after I'd refused him casual grazing on the Ladies' Meadows, misunderstanding, as it turns out, the restrictions imposed by the REPS plan on grazing another farmer's livestock. I remember asking whether it would cause him difficulty, whether he had enough grass in his own place for them, and he'd replied that he would get by with a bit of silage. By that stage in my pregnancy I was only listening with half an ear; otherwise, I think, I would have heard the catch in his throat.

The consensus among our farming neighbours was that Joe had not been himself all autumn. Several people had seen he was low. The doctor, someone said, had told Susie that depression was among the possible side effects of the drugs he'd been prescribed for his knee. Just before Christmas Joe had asked a friend to look after the gun he used to rig for blanks to scare the fox away. He'd said then that he didn't want it in the house, in case something went amiss. His friend took him to be referring to the last burglary they'd suffered, when Susie had been knocked down and beaten badly. Putting this information together with his demeanour over Christmas, it seems Joe had been thinking about putting an end to things for some time.

The dawn he had chosen was the day of our meeting, and this was a fact I had to face. The pension, along with the question of how we might lessen the demands of Joe's job, were to be the main topics of conversation, but of equal concern to me was the state of the lodge. Since March, Susie had been complaining of a draught coming in under the eaves in their bedroom. I had promised to send down roofers to replace the felt, fix the missing slates and do whatever was needed, but she would have none of it. 'Joe will do it,' she had said.

I had not really understood the cause of her resistance until the public health nurse, who was regularly visiting me to check Kim's progress, put me straight. 'Their conditions are awful, shocking, really,' she told me. 'But Susie is not going to let you or anyone else interfere because she's afraid the HSE will take Joseph from her if they think she cannot cope. Nothing I can say or do will change her mind.'

Any substantial work on the lodge also posed real logistical issues. As the council's planning consultant had indicated that day in the dining room, the lodge had been listed along with the main house in the County Development Plan. This meant that planning permission would need to be obtained for any renovations, and a conservation architect employed to supervise them. Never having got beyond the front room myself, I had learned from the nurse that the toilet installed by Joe drained to a cesspit behind the house. The bath was wedged into the kitchen. The water supply, like that of the main house, came directly from the stream. The lodge was overrun with mice. Originally a three-room structure, a fourth room had been added that merely integrated the external yard and privy with uninsulated walls of cinderblocks and a flat, felt roof. Susie had fallen several times on the uneven floor, the nurse told me. In short, the lodge needed to be gutted in its miniature entirety and then replumbed, rewired, reroofed and insulated before it could be made habitable by modern standards. How or where the Kirwans could be accommodated while this work was carried out was proving a real conundrum. So, too, was the question of how the works could be financed.

The trustees did not know what kind of tenancy agreement, if any, the Kirwans had. After the house had been conveyed to me, I called Charles's solicitor to ask his advice. As was often the case in these situations, he explained, the Kirwans tenanted the lodge under a caretakers' agreement. This afforded them lifelong occupancy, rent-free, so long as the property was kept up to the owner's satisfaction.

This conversation handed me a key to understanding Susie's persistent refusals of all help. The agreement that saw them housed in part-payment for their work functioned so long as they could maintain the lodge themselves, or pay for someone to do it, while they planned and saved for retirement. Charles had failed in not pushing Susie to make these plans and in allowing the lodge to fall into such a state of disrepair that it denied the Kirwans a proper standard of living when they needed it most. As Susie said, Master Charles could never say no to her, and as a result she had become trapped into relying on his personal loyalty. If Susie were to admit to me the state of the place, then according to the agreement she'd signed long ago I would have grounds to turf her and her family out of their home as inadequate caretakers. I hoped she knew me better than to suspect I'd do this, but her upright regard for the letter of the law meant I could not be sure. I'd introduced too many changes, was too fond of paperwork, relied on too many advisers, to be entirely trusted. Combined with her fears about Joseph's care and Joe's fears of redundancy, the Kirwans had become trapped in a feudal box that wouldn't allow them to admit their own vulnerability to anyone who might be able to help them. In his own way, Joe had realized all this but was unable to think his way through it. I could hardly blame him. 'How will it end?' he had asked. I still don't know the answer.

On the morning of Joe's funeral, the mountains turn out for him at Ballyroan: droves of neighbours from Kilmashogue, Tibradden, Montpelier and Glendhu. Many of my farming classmates from Glenasmole are there. I entrust Kim in his buggy to Mary's care and take my place with Susie at the top of the church. Colin goes on alone to the graveside in Cruagh while I return home to feed Kim. Joe is taken past the grave of his friend George Reid, the drayman, whose stone simply reads 'Move on!' – the catchphrase used to disperse those who stopped to chat outside his cottage at Rockbrook or take a glass of milk from his cows. Eddie, a former neighbour who was very close to Joe and Susie, releases two white doves above the grave; they will make their own way back to his home in Kilmacanogue.

'Did you see the doves?' Susie asks me later, and then she uses a word I've never heard her speak before: 'They were beautiful, they really were.' In her face, I catch the brief flicker of a private memory, before this extravagance is snuffed out and she returns to staring down the future with wet and unseeing eyes.

12.

Although the summer sunlight gild
Cloudy leafage of the sky,
Or wintry moonlight sink the field
In storm-scattered intricacy,
I cannot look thereon,
Responsibility so weighs me down.
W. B. Yeats, 'Vacillation'

January 2006

In Susie's front room I meet neighbours to whom I have waved
on the road without knowing their names. John arrives each
morning to set and light the fire and to collect Susie's list of
shopping and errands. Sometimes he brings Susie her favourite
treat of fish and chips, which she eats straight from the bag. In
the evenings, old friends who have been warded off these past
few years are welcomed back across the threshold to sit in by
the fire. When I call mid-morning with Kim in his sling, Susie
tells me news of other people's children, whom they have married, their complicated careers in Dublin or abroad. She is
determined to cope, and to show she is coping, confining her
grief and anxiety to the time when the door is pulled shut
behind her visitors and she can worry alone.

Neighbours and friends have told me they are concerned
about how Susie and Joseph will manage without Joe to drive
them to the supermarket on a Friday morning, or to the doctor

173

when required. The public health nurse visits them twice daily now, mornings and evenings, to assist their getting washed and dressed. Susie will not accept any other professional assistance. Nor, the nurse tells me, would a carer agree to work in the lodge in its current condition. She has arranged for Meals-on-Wheels to visit daily, but their carefully prepared foil containers are going straight into the bin, unopened. Susie prefers to cook up fries and mash the food with a fork or occasionally her own teeth before passing it on for her son, who has no teeth of his own, to swallow. Each morning, John sweeps up unlit matches and chunks of firelighter from the hearth carpet where Susie has dropped them in her attempts to rekindle the fire. One evening he found a pot boiled dry on the cooker, the ring still lit, the charred embers of the lunchtime potatoes burning blackly inside.

Two weeks have passed since Joe's funeral. Eight of us are assembled in the local health centre, sitting in a circle on hard plastic chairs, while Kim snores gently beside me in his car-seat. The public health nurse has gathered us for a crisis strategy meeting to discuss how the Health Service Executive can best provide care for the Kirwans. Her case-load cannot sustain the twice-daily visits to the lodge for ever. She needs other services to help alleviate the crisis and share the burden of finding the best way out of it for Susie and Joseph.

The chairman, who manages the HSE's disability services in the area, asks us to introduce ourselves in turn. I am greatly relieved by the range and rank of professionals in attendance and by how well they've been briefed on the case. The Kirwans' long-standing GP is here, along with a social worker for the elderly, who has yet to meet Susie and Joseph. A social worker from St Michael's House, a community-based care service for the intellectually disabled, sits beside me with her director of services; Joseph is already on their books, having attended their school many years ago for a brief period before his mother withdrew him. John is here as an advocate for Susie. When my turn comes round, I struggle to find the right terms to describe my relationship with the Kirwans before settling unhappily on 'concerned landlord and employer'.

One by one, the ethical knots I have been fumbling with in the dark are methodically untied. The first principle established is that Joseph and Susie should stay together for the time being, if at all possible. No one wishes to add the trauma of separation to the trauma of Joe's death. The ties of co-dependence must be loosened, but loosened gradually, for Joseph's sake, so that he can survive the transition to institutional care in the longer term. Susie will need to be supported in implementing a care plan for her son: this would include getting him ready to be collected and brought to St Michael's House for rehabilitation several times a week if they remain in the lodge. Susie's determination to stay there must be balanced with her son's right to some sort of future. St Michael's House undertakes to assess Joseph's developmental needs; Susie will have to weather a visit from the psycho-geriatrician. Once their capabilities have been assessed, the case team can decide how best to address the deficiencies of their current situation. With that, there is a pause, and I realize the chairman is waiting for me.

I hesitate, trying to find the right words to describe Susie's attachment to her home, despite the squalor. Charles's distress over the threat to their sun-porch has suddenly flooded to mind.

'The place is a kip,' John offers. He holds up his hand for all to see and counts off its faults one by one on his fingers: 'No bathroom, no proper kitchen, no mains water, no septic tank, the wiring I've fixed myself. The mice run through it and there's clutter everywhere. There are bars on the windows and the whole place is a hazard. Sure, there's a tank of kerosene sitting there within yards of the house and an open fireplace in the living room, and I'll tell you my fear – it's that some morning I go up to see Mrs Kirwan and find the whole place gone, burned to the ground, the way Joe's mother's was, God rest her, and they inside. They can't go on living there. It's not fit for animals.'

I feel myself flush with shame. Yet it comes as a relief to hear the condition of the lodge so plainly, and undeniably, inventoried.

I explain that the building's listed status will require me to seek planning permission for renovations on the scale suggested by John's inventory. Nor will it be easy to implement any modifications an occupational therapist might suggest to aid Susie's mobility. The fitting of handrails and ramps will have to comply with the guidelines set by conservation practice as well as the usual standards of health and safety. As it is, Susie has to use a combination of stick and furniture as her aids because the rooms are too tight to negotiate with a frame. Wheelchair access, which may soon be necessary, would require knocking down walls. For all these reasons, nothing at the lodge can happen quickly, and if and when it does, Susie and Joseph will have to move out for the duration of the works.

Those who haven't met Susie find it difficult to understand why she cannot be gently persuaded to move out of a home so obviously ill-suited to her needs, and into a nursing home alongside her son. Those of us who know her well struggle to convey the sheer force of her will to remain in the house where she was born, her last bastion of family, duty, honour and position.

The chairman allots tasks to everyone, and draws the meeting to a close.

★

'Come on now, Polly. That's it.' The ewe steps gingerly towards the edge of the platform and looks out at her sisters grazing below. Seán Cooney tugs the lever and two bars clamp in against her neck with a loud clatter. He retrieves the probe from the bucket of soapy water with his right hand and reaches in under the ewe's belly. 'Two,' he announces confidently with a glance at the screen. Peering over the top of the crush, I expect to see a shape familiar from Holles Street, but all I see is an ocean of static. I scrawl '2' next to the tag number I've jotted down and, exchanging my damp clipboard for an aerosol can, spray two red lines vertically across her rump. Seán releases the lever and the ewe hops down to join the others as Colin shunts the next one in.

With sixty-eight ewes to get through and a pair of novices to work with, Seán's not free with the chat. He arrived this morning at a bad moment, when we were trying to catch the last of the escapees from the first batch of ewes. We'd had them penned in underneath the archway that divides the top and middle yards at Cloragh when one of them jumped the wooden hurdles as cleanly as a racehorse. After that they all followed, trampling the gates down as they scarpered through the middle yard. I let Moss off the lead to give chase, scattering them further until Colin caught and roundly berated her for uselessness. Only then did I remember that Joe used to call this dog 'the ornament'.

It all seemed so straightforward yesterday. Our neighbour Pádraig – who got out of sheep after he'd figured that, if it took 6.66 sheep to make up one livestock unit, he'd be tending twenty-six and a half hoofs for the four of a suckler cow – arrived mid-morning with gates and hurdles from his own farm. 'There's some work in sheep,' he said, before urging Colin down through the gusting rain to the yard to set up a sheep race – a corridor of fences in which the ewes can be queued and inspected individually. It had been his idea to hire the scanner. 'I know Joe didn't hold with it but, Jesus, if you're lambing for the first time you don't want to be in up to your oxter counting feet.' The best plan, he reckoned, was to drive the sheep down through the archway to the lower yard, close over the huge tarred doors and herd them back up and into the old pens on the left. Each batch could then be herded back in through the archway doors and confined with hurdles in a holding pen. From there we could usher them individually into the race.

'Usher?' Colin queried sceptically.

'Well, call it what you will,' Pádraig conceded, with a laugh.

All fine in theory, grumbles Colin, today, but Joe's sheep aren't used to being penned. Twice this morning, he's been sent flying on the slippery cobbles trying to catch renegades, his temper not helped by his wife's suggestions of small improvements he might make to the race that he and our neighbour spent wet hours assembling.

When Seán arrived, manoeuvring his Jeep easily over the deep ruts in the track to Cloragh, I realized that becoming sheep farmers was going to entail a certain loss of face. Casting a practised eye around the yard, Seán picked up two small hurdles and made a new pen of one of the small, open sheds and stood close by. 'See if you can herd her up this way,' he called, nodding at the wild-eyed Cheviot dashing in and out of the broken machinery and briars. Colin flapped, the sheep moved forward; I flapped, she went into the pen. As she did so, Seán leaped over the side and wrestled her into a corner, one hand on her tail, the other twisting her head back onto her shoulder. Beaten, she allowed herself to be steered meekly back to rejoin the mêlée in the holding pen.

All in all, the scanning takes about an hour and a half. 'Sure next year,' Seán says, 'you'll have yourselves better organized.'

He reads out the final tally from the screen: 'You've thirty-nine singles, twenty-two twins and one with triplets, and six are empty. That's a lambing average of 1.26.' This is a little on the low side.

'What ram did you use?' he asks.

'A Texel,' I reply. 'Joe said he should have some spring in him.'

'Right enough, he did,' he says, happier now the job is done to dispense advice. 'All your male lambs should be good butcher lambs. But if you want to raise your average, try a Belclare next time, though you'll end up with triplets.' His eyes twinkle when I ask why that's a problem.

'A ewe has only two place settings like ourselves,' he says politely, 'so usually you'll end up with a pet on the bottle, and I gather you've one of those already.'

The day won't be finished till we herd the ewes carrying twins and the triplets over to the Nineteen Acres, those carrying singles to the Lawn, and the cast, or empty, ewes to the Shrubbery field where they can wait till we work out what to do with them. Each group, Seán says, will require different rations till we're due to start lambing on Paddy's Day. Before he goes, I pick up my clipboard and write down details of the feed we have to buy. 'You can get it delivered in bags of twenty-five kilos,' Seán says. 'That'd be the handiest way. Sure you can throw a couple of bags in the loader and away you go.'

Colin grimaces. There's no point in correcting Seán's mistaken impression that we own the blue tractor parked on the drive. It is Joe's tractor. I don't fancy trying to get Susie's permission to use it, even if we could switch the insurance to cover my husband as its inexperienced driver.

After Seán has gone, Colin and I sit down together on a hummock of rock in the middle of the yard while the sheep graze around us. 'I'd like the comfort of a body not my own,'

Colin says, leaning into my shoulder. His face is streaked with mud and sheep shit, and beneath the dirt there's pain from the fall he took earlier on the stones. He is exhausted. Every morning, he's brought Kim with him when he drops Mel to school, allowing me to recover an hour or two's sleep from the broken nights of feeding. And since Joe died, he has been out before it gets light to check if any sheep have become entangled in the briars or hogget wire. He has been working late, too, the green shade of his desk lamp signalling that preparation is under way for the term ahead. Yesterday *Practical Sheep Keeping* arrived from Amazon in the same parcel as Ernst Bloch's *The Spirit of Utopia*. Alongside Jean Baudrillard's *America*, his customer homepage now identifies *Sheep: The Remarkable Story of the Humble Animal that Built the Modern World* as a book he might also enjoy reading.

We have naturally discussed selling the flock. We could quit the REPS plan now, I've argued, and forfeit only the first year's payment and perhaps a fine. Although I still don't know, eighteen months on, how much we will be awarded for our Single Farm Payment, given the paucity of the subsidies claimed by Charles, it is unlikely to amount to much of a wage. If we lease out the land, none of our farm payments will be retained; on the other hand, neither will we have to fork out the costs of feed, fencing, equipment, and the contractors' fees for topping weeds and spreading lime. Without Joe and Susie's wages to pay, we could break even if we continued farming ourselves. But without Joe's help, and with two children and two academic careers to mind, I can't see how there will ever be enough slack in the day to accomplish all the intimate tasks of sheep husbandry so vividly described in the books on our bedside table. We could advertise for someone to help but, as Colin points out, it would be tricky enough to write the job description without knowing ourselves exactly what the job entails or how we'd supervise it. The extent and range of Joe's work is only just becoming apparent. Besides, we're not in a position to offer sufficient incentive for any likely candidates to leave the building trade. If we sell the sheep before they've lambed, we'll get half the amount we'd get selling them with lambs at foot in the summer. All things considered, it seems to make sense to give lambing a go. 'It's rare enough you get the chance to try something new when you're nearing forty,' Colin says bravely.

At Joe's funeral, a number of people offered to help. Few of them knew us well. Shortly after, Seán Jones, my REPS classmate from Glenasmole, came over with his dog, Duke, to round up the sheep in the Nineteen Acres and bring them into the old dipping pens. I put Kim in his sling and took Mel out to watch, and we all stood, astonished at how the dog could keep the sheep grouped together at the gap to the ford while the two men went off to gather the rest from the far corner. If a sheep so much as turned its head, Duke would circle round and hunker opposite the likely bolter, ears raised, nose down, till his opponent thought better of it. 'Can we get a sheepdog, a real sheepdog, like that?' asked Mel at my elbow.

'I think we may need to find a real shepherd first,' I said, as her father came into view.

But I did Colin a disservice. Down in the pens, Seán Jones showed him how to catch and turn a ewe upright onto her tail, wedge her firmly between the knees, and reach down over her shoulder to inject the Heptavac into the fold of loose skin between her back leg and udder. It took them the whole afternoon to vaccinate all sixty-eight against pneumonia and clostridial infections. Without Seán's encouragement and generous instruction, I doubt Colin would have felt confident enough to give lambing a go. When he came in for dinner that day, he was a changed man. 'It no longer feels like comedy,' he said, flopping into his chair at the table.

'Come on,' he says now, getting up stiffly from our rock in the yard. 'If you give me a hand getting this lot back into the pen you can go and relieve Mel of the baby. I'll run them back through the race to divide them up, and if you send her down, Mel and Moss can give me a hand herding the twins across to the Nineteen Acres.'

I do as he says and return to the house. I carry Kim over and sit near the window so that I can watch his father and sister herd the sheep across the wet pasture. Mel wears her grey hood up against the drizzle, Moss's lead tightly clutched as she switches right and back behind the striped flock to keep them from breaking, just as Duke had, while Colin runs alongside, urging them forward and calling back to Mel. They look united by the task, a good thing.

Later that night, the stove lit in our bedroom, the baby asleep in our bed between us, I ask Colin if, after the long day's labour, the pain and weariness of farming still seem worthwhile. 'In a funny way,' he answers, 'today made me think of my dad. All those years he worked as a machinist in Harland and Wolff and Rolls-Royce. The work today closed the gap a little, if you know what I mean.'

On the far side of the bed, the Compactom stands just a little ajar.

'You'll have to be like Mr Benn,' I say, nodding at it, 'and step into the changing room to try on a costume for your new adventure.'

'And what would that be?' he asks, smiling.

'I'd love to say a Stetson and cowboy boots, but round here I fear it means a flat cap, torn jeans, gumboots and an army surplus sweater.'

'I think I'll settle for a Barbour and a pair of waterproof trousers,' Colin says. There's a soft hiccup from between us, as Kim begins to stir.

'By the way,' I add, latching him on, 'Seán Cooney told me he bought his machine from Holles Street. You'd have thought he could have told us the sex.'

'Perhaps you just didn't ask him. Maybe you should next year.'

'Oh, next year, is it?' I say, raising an eyebrow.

The case team immediately follow up on their tasks. The job of persuading Susie to co-operate with the process has been shared between the public health nurse and Susie's friend John. I visit daily, but rely on John for news of how Susie is weathering the storm of intervention for she will not confide in me. He reports that she sent the psycho-geriatrician away with a flea in his ear, highly indignant that he should have the effrontery to ask her, in her own front room, to name the present Taoiseach. 'As if I could forget that Mr Ahern!' It took him some considerable time, he says, to calm her down. By the time the case chairman visits to discuss Joseph's care, she is more prepared. Much to his surprise, he finds her generally amenable to the idea of letting Joseph attend St Michael's House a few days a week, so long as someone can help her get him ready for their driver to collect.

In due course, the psycho-geriatrician reports back that Mrs Kirwan seemed sharp as nails on the day he visited. Apart from the poor hygiene evident in her personal appearance and her living environment, his assessment could find no grounds upon which to question her judgement. Unless Susie is deemed to be of 'unsound mind', there can be no question of the HSE overruling her choice of where to live. Yet it is clear to me that the HSE must assess Joseph's care independently of his mother's, and that if it takes making Joseph a ward of court to ensure he is living in suitable circumstances, they will do so – even if this means separating mother and son. Faced with this prospect, I agree to refurbish the lodge to provide accommodation suitable for them both, while Susie and Joseph are housed temporarily in a nursing home. When they return, the HSE will provide twenty-four-hour home care, while Joseph attends St Michael's as an out-patient.

This is a complicated solution to a complicated problem. There is no guarantee that Susie will be judged fit to move back into the lodge by the time the works are complete. She received treatment for breast cancer five years ago, and has since had skin cancers removed. Even if her health is good enough, the occupational therapist has expressed doubts as to whether the lodge can be made suitable for Susie, Joseph *and* an overnight carer, given that it is a listed building, which would have to be extended to provide a second bedroom. The solicitor once explained to me that the condition of the lodge gave me legal grounds to evict the Kirwans, should I ever need to. Effectively this would require the HSE to house them for the rest of their lives. But who could do this? When Charles died, I promised Susie that no one would ever ask her to give up Tibradden. And I won't now.

It is hard enough to ask them to leave temporarily, and to witness their departure. The day before St Valentine's, a neighbour from up the hill comes to collect Susie and Joseph, and drive them down to the nursing home in Dun Laoghaire where they will be roomed together while the lodge is renovated. As far as Susie's concerned, Dun Laoghaire – about six miles from here – could be Timbuktu; she has asked several times over the past few days where exactly it is and how long it takes to get there. This apparent lack of knowledge must be a sign of her distress; surely, at some stage in her life, she knew where the mail-boat docked, and from where the cattle-boat sailed. All morning, John has been inside trying to help them pack and to comfort Susie. 'I've done things this morning I should never have had to do,' he says, as we carry their suitcases out to the car.

Susie is dressed in her warmest black coat and the new skirt and jumper I bought her at Christmas. Joseph, too, is wearing his best. He peers around him at all the bags in the living room and shouts again for his twine. John goes out to fetch a length from the two bales he has put in the boot, the most important luggage of all. 'What will happen to my things? Who will look after them?' Susie asks again, as the neighbour goes out to pack up the car. I promise to store them carefully and bring her whatever else she may need. 'What about the furniture?' she asks. I tell her it will be moved to the coach-house, where some of our own is still stored. 'When will this work be finished?' she asks. I outline the whole process again, knowing that she is listening only for the unknowable date when she can return home. 'I'll never see Tibradden again,' she concludes. 'After all these years, I'm leaving Tibradden.' Beyond grief, her voice expresses rising indignation and incredulity that such a thing could come to pass.

'You will of course, Susie,' I tell her, but in truth it will be up to the case team to assess when and whether she and Joseph are capable of returning home.

When the car is packed, I help Susie up and steer her slowly out of the door. She has her keys in her hand. Joseph is already in the back seat, twisting the blue baler twine through his fingers. She reaches out to the doorjamb to steady herself, or so I think at first, but then I realize she is stroking it. It is a momentary gesture, a silent prayer from a woman who, I thought, had given up prayer long ago.

'Are you right now, Susie?' the neighbour asks gently, as she tucks the hem of her coat inside the car door. Susie, her eyes wet, says nothing. Beside her, Joseph presses his face to the window and chuckles. The car moves off through the gates.

John promises to call in later to see them settled; I will go tomorrow.

I release the brake on the buggy and bounce Kim back up the drive past the tractor shed. Are this morning's events the end Joe feared, or had the effort of imagining any end at all exhausted his failing energy? I wonder bitterly whether motive really counts for anything when the scene is the same as a nineteenth-century eviction: a house, poorly kept, reclaimed by the landlord, the tenant in tears, her suitcases lined up on the path outside for all to see as she and her son are ferried to the workhouse. 'You're not to blame,' Colin says, when he comes in from work and sees my face. But his assurance rings hollow to my ears, standing, as we are, shoulders bowed, in the place my ancestors built so sturdily.

13.

In March, the weather turns colder. Colin dons a furry hat with
ear-flaps before going out, a shepherd in wolf's clothing, which
he exchanges hastily for a suit before leaving to lecture his
Maynooth students on the complexities of the commodity fet-
ish. He is feeding the ewes twice daily now, and fixing fences
when he can. He and Mel have spent pointless days chasing
sheep into separate regiments only to wake and find that overnight they've regrouped through holes in the hedge. In
February, the hoggets strayed. We had assumed them to be
safely grazing the set-aside fields across the road until a neighbour called to the door to tell us she'd found them chewing
their way through the stretch of rough grazing she likes to
keep for the birds and wildlife. 'Your grandmother used to have
the place beautiful,' she said, with a nod at the weeds growing
up through the front steps. 'We used to come up every year to
see the rhododendrons, but I suppose they've gone.'

My husband, and hence the whole house, is beginning to
smell of sheep. It is not an unpleasant smell, reminding me of
the plain tubes of lanolin my grandmother used as hand-
cream, since rebranded as an 'essential', and costly, product
for breast-feeding mothers. In the evenings, after Kim has
been fed to sleep and Mel has been chivvied to bed, we slump
in the study, too tired to move, and try to read up on lambing.
The book's most alarming section is on abnormal presenta-
tions. Among the breech births and diagrams of how to deliver

triplets is a drawing of a prolapsed ewe which instructs the shepherd to wash the expelled uterus in a bowl of liquid detergent before returning it back inside. Oh, Lord, I empathize. No gas and air, no pethidine, and no epidural while a novice obstetrician rummages around your insides.

'"If the front hoofs can be seen but the lamb's head is turned back against the pelvis,"' I read out loud, '"attach ropes to its forelegs and return them to the uterus. Then reposition the head to lie between the forelegs and rope it, too, to prevent it inevitably" – yes, that's what it says, *inevitably* – "springing back into its original position. Then ease the head and legs into the birth canal and draw the lamb as for a normal presentation."'

Colin gulps. 'Simple, then.'

Ten days before lambing is due to start, our friend Siobhán comes to stay. She had written after Christmas asking whether the offer to spend some of her sabbatical with us was still open. It was, I replied cautiously, but a few things had changed. She was undeterred and, as usual, she surprised me. 'Lambing, hey? I come with some experience on that front.' While living in Mayo, she had often helped out on a friend's sheep farm. It had been a while ago, she said, but she was sure some of the shepherding knowledge remained.

And so, one Saturday approaching the ewes' due date, I copy out the list of essential lambing equipment from *Practical Sheep Keeping*, load the baby into the back of the Land Rover, seat my friend in the front and take the scenic route up and over the Dublin Mountains to Blessington. At the viewing point at Killakee, I pull over so Siobhán can take in the whole expanse of Dublin Bay. I point out the silhouette of the Mournes on the far horizon, a jet taking off over Portmarnock, the stringed harp of the Luas bridge at Dundrum and then the sight that impresses me most, Pádraig's cattle grazing the foreground below us in Castlerag. We drive on up over the Featherbed and I point to the overhang where one day, two years ago, I spotted Oliver Schurmann, our tenant in the walled garden, paragliding on the thermals. At Sally Gap, we turn right and pull in again. The cold morning sun has turned the dry sedge in the Coronation Plantation the colour of gilded silver, stamped blackly in several places by the surviving Scots pines.

Viewed from this hinterland, Tibradden no longer seems anomalous, a farm washed up by the city in some inter-tidal zone. From here the mountains roll down into the valleys, a progressively greener carpet replacing the heather underlay as you descend towards sea level. Instead of being a bulwark of the Pale – a bastion of some sort against the hill rebels, as Thomas Hosea Guinness thought when, in 1867, he led a battalion of the Scots Greys to quash the Fenians in Tallaght – Tibradden is more naturally a staging post where city and mountain meet.

Our destination is an agricultural suppliers housed in a breeze-block bunker on the outskirts of Blessington. The lambing implements they stock do not look sturdy enough for the tasks ahead. Siobhán picks up a blue forked tube with a retractable string that looks like a catapult and puts it confidently into the basket. 'Lambing aid,' she whispers. 'The loop goes over the hoofs or head.'

I am impressed. 'See if you can find the castration rings,' I whisper back, 'and a matching elastrator.' A packet of what look like orange Cheerios and a version of a tin-opener join the tube in the bottom of the basket. 'What do you think this is?' I ask Siobhán, picking out a red plastic T with ties at either end.

'Haven't a clue,' she answers. 'Put it in anyway.'

Stomach tube and syringe, iodine, powdered glucose, Lamlac replacement milk powder, disposable calving gloves that extend past my armpit, a tub labelled 'Magniject', two feeding bottles and teats, in which Kim takes a sudden interest, new dagging shears, a drenching gun – all go into the basket. 'Lubricant,' I read from the list. 'How much lubricant do you think we'll need?' Three washing-up bottles' worth, we decide, to be on the safe side. At the till, I spy a stack of neat fluorescent envelopes. 'Look,' I say, unfolding one to stick my fingers through the four little leg holes. 'It's a high-vis vest for lambs!' By now we are giggling like girls. I shy away back down the aisle until I am sufficiently sober to pay the stern-faced cashier.

The first lamb is born four days later, a Wednesday night, five days ahead of schedule. By Thursday evening, there are twelve. Early the next morning, Colin and Mel depart for the weekend to Hull to see Mel's mother – a trip that was scheduled carefully so that they'd be back in time for lambing. By lunchtime, we have eighteen lambs.

Kim wakes me long before sunrise on Saturday morning. I feed him sleepily, marvelling at how he has grown. His dark hair is gradually lightening. I think he will be blond, as his daddy was as a child. The last thing I want to do on this cold March morning is to stomp off in my gumboots to look for labouring sheep. But Colin is away and it is my watch. I tiptoe into Siobhán's bedroom and reluctantly pass over my warmly bundled baby for her to mind while I head outside.

It is chilly downstairs. I feel old as I start to pile on the layers. Outside there's a roar in the trees, but it's not as wild as it might be in March. The torch spills a bowlful of light as I lurch sideways down the grassy slope and into the field. The sheep are huddled beneath the lime tree against the roar of the wind that has the clouds marching pinkly above the city below. One or two sound a sleepy alert and get to their feet when I turn in their direction. I am the night nurse turning on the ward lights at an inappropriate hour. At the bottom of the field, I spy a scrap of white out on its own. I stumble down to it and put my finger in its cold mouth expecting to find it lifeless, but the jaw moves slightly in a pathetic attempt to suckle. I set it back down for a minute to search for its mother in the gorse, trying to run through the things I need to do if I find her labouring, but all the sheep appear to be sheltering as a flock. The lamb is barely able to shiver. I go back, pick it up, tuck it inside my coat. Its head lolls sideways. It doesn't look good.

Back in the kitchen I find a cardboard box and set the lamb down by the radiator while I heat the hopsack the midwives recommended I use for back pain during my own pregnancy. One of the textbooks has a chart showing what to do in cases of hypothermia. 'Over 5 hours old, head down; cannot swallow,' it reads mid-way down. 'Give an intraperitoneal injection of glucose (fig. 90) then warm.' Figure 90 shows a needle pointing to a spot beside the lamb's navel. 'Insert the needle at an angle of 45 degrees.' This is precisely why I never wanted to be a nurse. Following the directions on the tub, I make up a warm glucose solution in a Pyrex jug, trying to guess how heavy the lamb is by comparing it to Kim. Between two and three kilos, I decide. I fetch Mel's ruler and a felt-tip marker and stretch out the lamb on the kitchen table to mark the spot. There's only a shallow flutter in its tiny lungs. I unwrap the syringe, carefully unclick one of the needles and fiddle it on. 'There should be no resistance – withdraw if there is,' the book warns. Stretching the skin as best I can I put the tip of the needle against the black dot. I have to push it quite firmly to penetrate the skin, and then it's in what I pray is the body cavity. I squeeze in 25 mls and take out the syringe. The lamb appears to be breathing still.

I have overheated the hopsack in the microwave and now fear burning my patient. What I need, according to the book, is an infrared lamp, but somehow this got omitted from my shopping list. My eyes turn to the fan oven. I take my largest baking tray, line it with newspaper, lay the lamb snugly on its side, its limp head propped on the rim, then wrap the tray in a tight blanket of tinfoil before lifting it onto the bottom shelf at 80°C.

After half an hour, I notice that the lamb has started shivering, a good sign, according to the book. A little while later I hear the dry rustle of tinfoil as it stirs in its survival bag. 'Hello, Lazarus,' I say, as its eyes open weakly. I pick it up and cradle it on my lap to examine it more closely. Warmed-up lamb, I discover, smells disconcertingly akin to roast lamb, something James Herriot never mentioned. Feeling pathetically pleased with myself, I fetch from the freezer an ice-cube bag filled with beestings, the colostrum that Pádraig saved for us during calving and told me to freeze for use in emergencies. I pop three orange ice-blisters out of their plastic and into a beaker, which I then set inside a bowl of boiling water till the beestings have defrosted, before adding a drop of cod-liver oil. Joe once advised doing this in the days when such a recipe was a point of idle interest, a way of making conversation in the absence of anything else to say.

The next task facing me is stomach-tubing the lamb. The key is to avoid passing the tube into the lungs, where any milk will drown my patient instantly. I unwrap the tube and carefully pass the clear end over the back of my index finger, which presses down the tongue. The lamb's sharp teeth come as a sore surprise: I'd assumed all new-born herbivores just sucked with their gums. Its small body absorbs more tube than I would have thought possible. I wet my top lip and pucker against the open end to feel any whisper of a breeze from its windpipe that would tell me I'd misfed the tube. I'm not certain. I decide to withdraw it and try again. The second time, the lamb opens its eyes and softly bleats what I take to be a protest. I try again. This time, it seems more comfortable, chewing a little on the plastic. The beestings smell like cream on the turn but the lamb doesn't seem to mind as I squirt down two full syringes. The chart tells me it needs a full litre in the first twenty-four hours to survive. When I've finished feeding, I find some old towels and nestle the lamb in the cardboard box under the clothes rack in the boiler room. It's time now to return upstairs and attend to my own child.

By the time Colin and Mel return on Sunday night, Siobhán and I have become dab hands at neo-natal care: spraying mother and lamb with matching numbers, castrating male lambs and docking tails by fitting the little orange rings onto them with the elastrator. In truth, because of Kim's feeds, Siobhán does more than her fair share of this work. We have not had to deliver any lambs ourselves yet – the mothers have managed without our assistance. Still, there is a palpable sense of pride that twenty-six more lambs have been born on our watch.

The next night, Colin comes in from his rounds after supper to say that one of the ewes with twins out the front needs assistance. Mel agrees to baby-sit her sleeping brother so I can gather together the various implements and troop off after Colin and Siobhán into the dark.

When we reach the ewe, the lamb's head is already out, visibly swollen and with its tongue poking out. It looks like it's choking. Colin rolls up his right sleeve to put on the long calving glove, while Siobhán grips the ewe at the forequarters to try to keep her upright. I'm given the easy task of holding the torch and passing implements. I try to remember what the book said about lambs that present head first – something about pushing the head back in, then sorting out the legs to draw out the front hoofs.

If my own labour were not so recent, the ensuing struggles of man and beast might seem comical. Each time Colin pushes the lamb's head back in, the next contraction pops it out. After some minutes, it is clear that the book method is not going to work. Perhaps, Siobhán suggests, if a finger could be got in past the head, there might be a chance of hooking the front two hoofs with the lambing aid. Released from its wrapper, the blue plastic tube looks even more like a toy. Siobhán murmurs reassurance, although I think Colin needs it more than the ewe, as he loops the rope around his gloved fingers and tries to fumble in through the polo-neck of the vulva stretched tight around the lamb's ears. The ewe strains against him; she is panting heavily now.

Eventually, Colin manages to get two fingers inside and then his whole hand slides in suddenly until his wrist disappears beneath the lamb's head. The lambing aid has slipped and is dangling uselessly from his elbow like some sort of charm bracelet. Colin's face contorts with pain each time the ewe contracts. I dare not say anything. Later he'll tell me the pelvic bones felt like knives slicing across his knuckles.

The cry of a lamb down the field momentarily catches my attention. It sounds so like Kim. The torch dips and Colin swears. His head is twisted sideways as he gropes for something identifiable inside the ewe. We stand there for what seems an age, waiting, before his face suddenly relaxes and he draws a front hoof forwards. The lamb now looks as if it's peeking out of a woolly porthole for one last view. Colin reaches back in and, by twisting the head a little sideways, fetches out a second black hoof. He stands to straighten out his back for a minute. 'That's it now, I think,' he says, with some satisfaction. He bends again and takes a tight grip on each hoof and pulls steadily downwards. With a tremendous gush of liquid, the hot body finally slides to earth with a thud.

We stand back, the sense of victory fading as we watch the ewe attempt to nuzzle her big lamb to life. Siobhán crouches down next to the limp creature. With a handful of grass, she begins to brush away the amniotic fluid from around its nose, then rubs its wet flanks briskly up and down. 'Come on, come on,' she mutters, but there is no sign of the lamb breathing. She sits back for a moment and looks up at us, her eyes shining with determination. 'Would you mind if I . . . ?' she begins to ask, but Colin is already nodding, so she picks the lamb up by its hind legs and, stepping back from the mother, starts to swing it heavily from side to side.

And there it is suddenly, the convulsion and tiny cough as the lamb takes its first breath. The cord must have kept it alive through all that straining. It seems astonishing that life can be so stubborn. I'd never imagined I would ever witness birth from this angle. Siobhán sets the lamb down. We crowd round to see its clammy ribcage heave in and out before the ewe noses us away to inspect her offspring for herself. A little while later the second twin is delivered alive. We pen them in together at the front of the house and return to the kitchen, jubilant.

The night's work has settled a score. My rescued lamb survived less than twenty-four hours despite being fed as the book instructed. Although I understood now that it had been too small to stand a proper chance, I couldn't help wondering whether a more experienced nurse might have coaxed it to thrive.

The lambing and all the drudgery leading up to it have changed my relationship with where we live. There is a community of interest in these fields that is shared among those who work here. Colin and I stop on the road to greet neighbours, who ask us how we're getting on and tell us of farming triumphs or losses of their own. Others share news of an order for feed or fertilizer we might like to come in on. The phone numbers of contractors, shearers, fencers, those with a truck who'll drive sheep to mart, are passed on with recommendations, scraps of advice or tales attached. For the first time, living here, I feel properly local.

On our third wedding anniversary, at the end of April, Colin and I take Kim out to the walled garden after breakfast. While we've been lambing, Oliver and his employee, Michael, have been labouring hard to transform the jungle into a nursery with gravelled paths and wooden frames of perennials laid out according to their needs: sun, semi-shade and full shade. A new bed has been dug along the line of the path that used to run between the gooseberry bushes and sweet peas. It has been planted with grasses and tall thistles and *Verbena bonariensis*, which Oliver promises will attract tortoiseshell butterflies to its bright mauve flowers in midsummer. At the far end, where peaches used to ripen under glass, they have set up a potting shed, and Michael invites us in to see the seedlings he is nurturing under gauze-covered cloches. His taste in plants tends towards unshowy woodland varieties: the smaller and greener the flower the better. At night he stays up late in the hut that Oliver brought over from Stocking Lane and rebuilt with his friends from Germany. A long piece of plywood has been set on top of plastic fruit crates stacked three high to serve as a desk. Here he works on his own pet project: a horticultural compendium of the genus *polygonatum*, to which the arching Solomon's seal belongs.

Colin and I sit down on makeshift benches under the apple trees and lay a blanket on the pebbles so that Kim can watch the sun vanish and reappear through the fronds of the tree fern. It is good to sit here drinking tea together: we haven't had much time to talk these past few months and will have even less when I return to work next week.

'Now we've survived lambing,' I ask my husband, 'would you consider selling the sheep? It would probably make better financial sense to lease out the land.'

He reaches for my hand instead of answering. I'm surprised to see his Adam's apple bob up and down, as it does when he's upset. When he's ready, he looks at me, and says, 'We could, but I'd be devastated.'

'But why?' I ask incredulously, thinking of all the lone hours he has spent trudging through the cold and the dark, all the unprofitable effort of shepherding. Then I remember and ask more gently, 'Is it because of Joe?'

'Partly.'

'In a way you've done it for him, haven't you? You've seen out the season he started. But that doesn't mean we have to continue farming.'

Colin is still searching for words. 'Yes, but it's more than that. I know it sounds odd, but if I don't get to see a whole year through from start to finish, I think I'll feel like I've failed.' He hushes my rising protest and continues: 'When we first came to live here with Charles, I always felt a visitor. Your sense of place was so strong I couldn't find my own way to participate in it.'

It is, I tell him, what always worried me most about coming to live at Tibradden – that his own story would become eclipsed by my family's and that he would come to resent the place I loved.

'Ssh. I know. It's not like that.'

I say nothing, waiting for my husband to start again.

'You used to feel on the outside of my family, and then Mel came to live here. And you have accepted her as your responsibility, whatever the difficulties of being a stepmother. I don't mean to equate my children with sheep, but by taking over the farming from Joe, I feel as if I have more of a right to live here because of that work. It's becoming my place too. Does that make sense?'

I nod. It does. Working the farm confers a sense of belonging in a way that ownership by birth or history cannot.

Colin gathers up Kim. Our son waves his arms and laughs; his giggle is still the most optimistic sound I've ever heard. As we go back up towards the wooden door that leads to the house, I spy a clump of white violets among the pots in the section for shade-loving plants. 'Viola Joseph Kirwan', reads the label. I wave my thanks to Michael, who propagated them at my request from the clump Joe once identified as the last surviving ones planted by the Colonel.

14.

May 2006

From the front steps of Susie's nursing home, I can see an array of sails shining beyond Dun Laoghaire harbour in the hazy summer sun. There must be a regatta on. A Filipina nurse admits me, and stands by while I sign in. Susie, she says, is with Joseph in the conservatory. They've just had lunch. The nurse walks ahead of me along the corridor, and down the steps, where I find Susie and Joseph sitting on the chintz-covered suite, watching television. 'Ah, Miss Selina,' Susie says, without enthusiasm, 'so you've come to see me.'

'Yes, and I've brought the baby to see you too.' I unclip Kim from the car-seat and set him down on the floor next to my carrier-bag of peace offerings. Joseph squints hard at the baby and then, scrunching up his nose, squints harder at the bag beside him. He has spotted the strawberries. Quickly, before anyone can take them away, his hand goes out and pops one, stalk and all, into his mouth. He gums it happily.

His mother is not so easily mollified. 'No, thank you,' she replies, when I offer her the tub. Her gaze returns pointedly to the window. Joseph's remains fixed on the strawberries.

This is my first visit since I received a solicitor's letter, written on Susie's behalf, about six weeks ago. Until then, I had visited regularly, bringing tales of lambing and whatever scraps of local news I could glean from our neighbours. After a disastrous first night spent in separate rooms, when Joseph roared the place down, mother and son were accommodated together in a large twin room on the top floor with their own television and en-suite bathroom. The bale of twine was given pride of place on the middle shelf of the wardrobe. Susie told me she liked the food and was complimentary about the kind efforts of the owners, a couple of former psychiatric nurses, and the staff to settle them in. The other residents, she said, weren't the kind of people you'd want to talk to, most of them being plain doo-lally.

During the day, she and Joseph have the conservatory to themselves, and when it isn't cold they sit out in the garden by a flowerbed, currently ablaze with orange montbretia and yellow roses. Susie has had her hair cut and her nails trimmed, and she looks about ten years younger than she did when she left the lodge. Joseph started attending St Michael's House in his second or third week here. Whatever they do there, and she doesn't understand what it is at all, she has complained it is too much for him. He comes home tired and she finds him very hard to control. But, she says, since it is what those people want and they call the shots so long as she is living here, she supposes she has little choice but to go along with it.

Susie conceded that I would not be able to begin work on the lodge while we were lambing. But as soon as March was out, the question of when she might return home came to dominate my visits. Her suspicion is that in her hour of greatest need I am abandoning her and her son to the care of strangers, a fate to which she could never have dreamed herself condemned by a member of the family she has served for so long.

This is unfair. Despite the broken nights and a difficult return to work, I have interviewed a succession of architects about redesigning the lodge. Patricia O'Rourke, our weekly housekeeper, and I also spent a grim two days clearing it out.

Mice had been through every drawer ahead of us, and the soft record of the family's life together – letters, photographs, certificates – had been chewed into flitters for bedding. We discovered nests in the sofa and in the armchairs Susie had asked me to store. Nothing had been washed for a long, long time. We salvaged all the personal items we could in black sacks and suitcases, but most of the furniture was beyond salvation and we had to consign it to a skip. As Patricia said, the more you saw of how they had been living, the harder it was to imagine how they could possibly cope again on their own.

But this is what Susie has spent the past few months campaigning for. The solicitor's letter stated that his client, Mrs Kirwan, was claiming 'adverse possession' of the property she had maintained at her own expense for over fifty years and from which she considered herself to have been unlawfully evicted on 13 February last. He was now seeking independent confirmation of how the renovation works were progressing and stated that Mrs Kirwan expected to be restored to her property within weeks.

The letter arrived without warning, and its recourse to squatters' rights came as a surprise. Throughout our discussions of Joe's pension, Susie had often referred proudly to her 'accountanant', but in three years I had never once heard her mention a lawyer. Nor had she or Joe ever expressed any uncertainty before about who owned the lodge. It was, I recognized, some achievement to engage and brief a solicitor from the confines of a nursing home. It suggested the psycho-geriatrician's report was a more accurate assessment of Susie's mental capabilities than some of the case team had thought.

I forwarded the letter to Charles's solicitor, who replied in due course that the caretaker's agreement meant Susie had established no such entitlement, but that I would have no objection to her moving back into the lodge once the HSE judged it feasible. In the meantime, he stated that I would like to continue my visits to Mrs Kirwan and her son, if the same were acceptable to her. Word that Susie would be prepared to receive me came through a week ago.

We converse awkwardly, the silences made bearable only by the distraction of Kim's antics. Just as things are beginning to brighten up a little, we're interrupted by a care assistant who comes in carrying Joseph's coat over her arm. The taxi to take him to St Michael's House is waiting outside. Susie is not pleased.

'Excuse me!' she objects, her voice rising shrilly. 'He's only to go out two days a week. Sure he was at that place yesterday. He's not due to go again. You'll have to tell that man to go away.'

The assistant flashes me a practised smile to communicate she's been through this before. She advises Susie to take it up with the chairman of the case conference, who is due to visit later this week to review Joseph's progress with her.

'No one told me of the change in plan. I count for nothing. It was to be two days, not three or four.'

But whatever his mother thinks, the sight of his coat has transformed Joseph. Grabbing it, he marches with straight-forward purpose for the conservatory door and starts banging on the glass to get out. The noise provokes a torrent of repri-mands from Susie, which Joseph ignores. Wisely, the assistant abandons the discussion to open the door before the glass pane shatters. As Joseph disappears up the stairs, with a speed I've never seen him demonstrate before, it is clear that, whatever his mother says, the trip to St Michael's House is a welcome one.

The sudden commotion has frightened Kim. I pace up and down, trying to soothe his loud cries. Susie has balled her hanky in her fist and is fighting back tears at yet another defeat. I feel an intense pity for her.

Joseph is not due back till dinner-time. Outside the sun is shining.

'Come on,' I say, hauling her to her feet. 'How about an ice-cream?'

Susie says she has never before seen Killiney Bay, so this is where we will go. 'Oh, yes, I've heard of that place all right,' she says, as we pass through Glasthule. I find it hard to credit how little Susie has strayed from the tracks worn through south County Dublin in a farming lifetime. She perks up on the outskirts of Dalkey, where she remembers her father taking her fishing in a sea-pool many years ago. 'Pat Kenny lives somewhere near here,' she volunteers unexpectedly. As we approach the Vico Road, a bitter note creeps into her voice: 'Ah, yes, this is where all the moneyed people live. Millions, it must cost, millions to buy a house here! Where do they get the money from, Miss Selina? That's what I'd like to know!' I point out a few celebrity landmarks and she shakes her head with keen disapproval at their big gates and high walls.

'I hear they're to build flats on top of Superquinn in Ballinteer,' she says vehemently, daring me to confirm the worst. 'I never did like Tesco's. I hear they give you spanners now at Superquinn to get the money out of you when you're going round.'

It takes me a few minutes to work this out. 'Scanners, Susie, a kind of computer for reading the prices.'

'Oh, is that it?' There's a long pause as she notes the correction. Eventually she says, 'I suppose you'll be selling Tibradden?' Her tone lumps me in firmly with the 'moneyed people'.

'I doubt it very much,' I say.

'I hear Featherstone's have sold their golf course. To some man for houses, I suppose.'

'You're better informed than I am, Susie.'

'They'll be building houses on the Nineteen Acres next.'

I pull in to the Killiney Hill Stores to buy two Magnums, then circle back along the Vico Road to find a bench where we can sit and admire the view of the bay. Kim sleeps in his car-seat while Susie slurps away at her ice-cream. I point out the local landmarks: the Big Sugarloaf, the little one beside it, Bray Head jutting out at the end there, Dalkey Island straight ahead. 'Oh, yes, yes,' says Susie, breaking off big chunks of ice-cream with her fingers, the chocolate flaking onto her navy skirt where it slowly melts. 'Isn't the air marvellous? You'd know you were by the sea.'

It's only half past three, but Susie wants to return straight home. It is clear that being away from Joseph has made her anxious, although what she says is that she doesn't want to keep 'them people' waiting to give her her dinner. I have hardly pulled up on the road outside the home when she hares out of the passenger side. 'Hold on a second,' I say, as I struggle to release my seatbelt, 'and I'll see you in.'

'Ah, don't you trouble yourself, Miss Selina, I'll walk to the door myself.' I open my door, and begin to get out, but she calls firmly, 'I'm fine, thank you,' making her own way round the bonnet onto the pavement. She steadies herself against the railing, pulls herself upright and, with colossal effort, steers herself resolutely up the wrong driveway towards the apartment block next door.

Only then does it occur to me that we might as well have spent the past hour sitting in the car park of Susie's beloved Superquinn, for all she has seen of the view. There is nothing for it but to go in pursuit and rescue her as tactfully as I can. 'You might find this way easier, Susie. The ground's a bit uneven over there.' Losing confidence, she allows me then to take her elbow and guide her back round to the nursing home's front door. The nurse who opens it bows respectfully, and Susie unbends a little as she is ushered inside.

'Will you let me know soon, Miss Selina, what the word is on my house?'

In early June, the council's conservation officer inspects the lodge to determine what work can be commenced in the absence of planning permission. We pick our way gingerly through Susie's rooms. The bars on the small windows let in little daylight. Lit by a bare bulb, the bedroom walls are stained and chipped above the concrete floor. It looks like a place where a crime has been committed.

The conservation officer is a compassionate woman who is shocked by what she sees: the privy with its uneven floor, the bath in the kitchen, the unplastered cinderblock walls. I explain the situation as best I can – how, whatever we might think, this is the home Susie was born into and to which she longs to return. I explain how the terms of her tenure, and the paralysing shame my uncle shared, combined to trap her and her husband within their own limitations and the limitations of this place. She listens keenly, but I suspect that her sympathy for these complexities struggles to overcome the brute facts of the sour light, the soiled walls and the smell of rotten waste. The scale of works required to make this building habitable means I will definitely have to obtain planning permission. Once an application goes in, the council usually decides the outcome within twelve weeks. She would expect, however, that because the building is listed, additional information might be sought from my architects, in which case the process would be delayed further.

We step outside and breathe in deeply. It will not be easy, she warns, to facilitate disabled access without removing the entry and widening doorways throughout, and if we do go to this trouble, she would advise we think beyond the needs of the present occupant and consider adding a significant extension.

Few people nowadays are prepared to occupy the cramped quarters where once whole families were reared. Whatever work we undertake, we should take the opportunity to remove the inappropriate additions made by Joe: the breeze-block extension, the iron bars, the PVC windows and, above all, the tacked-on sun-porch. Gate-lodges, she finishes brightly, were designed to show passers-by what lay at the end of the avenue, to present the Big House in miniature, so it would be nice to have it once more looking well.

Soon after this, I obtain the number of the man who recently bought the old Prosser yard opposite our back gate. A small modern bungalow fronts the lane as part of the property, and it appears to be vacant. Perhaps, I think, he might be prepared to let it out for a reasonable sum so that Susie and Joseph can return to the neighbourhood while we await planning permission and then renovate the lodge.

The new owner turns out to be a joiner who has bought the place to house his workshop, which he intends shortly to relocate from Inchicore. The bungalow, he says, will become his new office, so he's afraid he can't help me out on this occasion.

A few days later, he rings back. The old lady's predicament has stuck in his mind. Would a log cabin be of any use to me, he asks. He and his team built it themselves from scratch to an authentic American design, with cedar timbers and cross-poles at each corner. He tells me it is well insulated and cosy, and that you could fit two bedrooms into it, although they'd be small. As a matter of fact, he's calling from it now, for the cabin houses his offices in his current yard. With the bungalow up above at Tibradden he'll have no use for it; considering all the work they put into it, he'd like to see it go to a good cause.

I find Gerry Farrell's yard at the end of a cul-de-sac on the edge of St Michael's estate in Inchicore. There is no missing the log cabin. It is set on top of his flat-roofed workshop as if perched on a mountain ledge, surrounded by blocks of council flats that tower above it. The setting is so incongruous it makes me laugh out loud.

Gerry invites me in, and at first glance the cabin seems the ideal solution. Inside it feels bright and warm, secure and dry. Gerry points out the solid maple floor, the double-glazing, the skylight. There's a bathroom with shower and toilet, and, off the main room, a kitchenette. The stud walls can be positioned whichever way we like. At 580 square feet, it's larger than the gate-lodge. Whether I take it or not, the cabin has to be dismantled; if I pay for the transport, I can have it for nothing. All I'd have to do is pour the concrete slab and pay the cost of rebuilding it. Best of all, being a temporary structure, it should not require planning permission. It is an extraordinarily generous offer. 'If you want it, you'll have to let me know in the next few days,' Gerry says. 'The developer wants this place cleared by Monday fortnight.'

Field by field, the farms around us are being sold. It is more than a year since Major McDowell rang me about the fence between our properties. He seems embarrassed when he rings again to tell me that he has sold all bar the sixteen acres around his house to Bernard McNamara, one of the most high-profile property developers in the country. Over the past six months McNamara's company has amassed at least a hundred acres around the junction of Kilmashogue Lane and Tibradden Road, ostensibly for the purpose of developing a golf course.

I have my doubts about whether a golf course is what McNamara really intends to build at St Thomas. It seems to me that this idea, dangled in negotiations, might be a way of sugaring the deal for landowners who are reluctant to see their well-farmed acres turned into a housing estate. There is nothing permanent about golf. Dun Laoghaire Golf Club was re-zoned for housing in the last County Development Plan, and already the JCBs have moved onto the fairways.

Driving home from work one day recently, I heard a cock-sure voice on the radio speak of all the 'derelict fields' he could see lying idle either side of the M50. It was criminal, the developer asserted, not to re-zone them for housing when young couples were forced to commute from as far away as Longford to hold down jobs in the capital. The presenter seemed to agree: Dublin's green fields were a luxury that might have to be sacrificed if young people like him were to lead normal family lives.

Now that St Thomas's fields have been sold – the amphi-theatre looking up to Tibradden, the ruins of Henigan's house at the bottom of the Nineteen Acres, both gone – I wonder how long we can hold out. As things stand, our fields form part of an agricultural enclosure that is largely hidden from the outside world. If a big residential development were per-mitted in our valley, we would lose that sense of place. Housing would also introduce the nuisances encroaching sub-urbia brings to farming communities: dog-attacks, fly-tipping, trespassers. If this is to be the future, we may need to be prag-matic and ensure we are not left marooned on the moral high ground.

In late summer, a man from Bernard McNamara's company arrives in a smart car, accompanied by the estate agent who valued Tibradden for probate. Once again, the dining-room table is covered with maps. Mr Noble, the developer's emis-sary, stabs his finger at the fields his company is interested in, and the estate agent identifies them by name: the Nineteen Acres (so sized by its old Irish measure – it is, in fact, thirty-three statute acres) and the field we use for silage, called the

Lower Lawn, or locally, 'the bus-stop field', which amounts to nine acres located below our front field. They would be interested in purchasing the full forty-two acres, or whatever portion of it I would be prepared to sell.

Mr Noble explains that they hope to tempt a nearby golf club to relocate here by offering them a brand-new eighteen-hole course as part of a deal whereby the club would sell its existing course, which lies within the M50, for housing. He seems very confident that the club will accept the package. 'What if they don't?' I ask. There are a number of other sporting organizations they have their eye on, he replies, and this rings true: all over the city, clubs are pocketing sweet promises of new clubhouses and better facilities if they'll only move quietly out beyond the city limits and leave their playing fields to the builders. What if I convey the land on a long lease with a clause restricting its use to solely sporting purposes? Would his company consider this a basis for negotiation?

His ready agreement comes as a surprise. He adds, 'We're playing the long game.'

We go outside. He pulls on the gumboots Colin has fetched him and we cross over the stream to the Nineteen Acres. The grass is high but our lambs are thriving on the brow of the hill. It is sunny and the field looks glorious with the swallows dipping low.

Back at the house, I told Mr Noble that there was no prospect of selling the Lower Lawn, as it is too close to the main house. But I am willing to consider selling some portion of the Nineteen Acres. There would have to be a buffer zone between McNamara's land and the stream where I hope Kim will play when he's older, as my brother and I did.

I spy a hare watching us from the top corner near the old redoubt.

'When I was a Cub Scout, I used to camp up here at Larch Hill and think I was out in the deepest countryside,' Mr Noble comments amicably, with a nod to the trees behind us.

'You were,' I reply.

Aware that I am taking advantage of his need to humour me, I point out the hare and then the ravens nesting in the tall cedar, the heron tracking towards Marlay ponds like a balsa-wood aeroplane. I find I can't help myself. All the time I'm trying to imagine this great expanse ploughed up by diggers. Buttercups and purple thistles are melting into the waving meadow of rye, fescue, brome and timothy. Ahead of us the Eleven Acres has been cut for silage, the fluorescent after-grass already shining through. The estate agent, the Major, my own father, too, all suggest that a golf course, its fresh green carpet undulating between shrubs, is not the worst fate for these acres. And we need the money.

On our way back to the house, the developer says, 'If you enjoy rural life so much, why not sell this place for a fortune and move down to the real country in Kildare or Wicklow?'

The question somehow communicates annoyance with the shit and the flies and the hole in his boot he discovered while crossing the stream. Perhaps he is frustrated, too, that such a prime piece of real estate should come freighted with sentiment and heritage, the kind of soft nonsense that scuppers a deal. And in the words he didn't say – 'Kildare or Wicklow, *where your sort belong*' – I hear the familiar echo of historical resentment that often blindsides my conversation with strangers.

Local word has it that I'm 'dumping the Kirwans into some class of a wooden hut'. My attempts to reassure Susie that the means I have found for getting her back to Tibradden is not some shack, but a log-house of the kind Colin and I had once thought to build for ourselves in the Shrubbery, have obviously been unsuccessful. 'How long will it take before it's ready, Miss Selina?' she asked dubiously, after squinting at the pictures I'd shown her. Not long, I told her. The sections of the cabin were now on site. Unless the planners throw up problems about drainage, we just have to lay a foundation slab and wait for it to set before inviting the carpenters back. She delivered her verdict with a sniff. 'Ah, well, to return to Tibradden after all these months spent here is what I want.'

The HSE have agreed to support the Kirwans' move to the log-house. It would be a simple matter to fit out the interior according to the guidelines laid down by an occupational therapist. But the conservation officer unexpectedly throws up an obstacle. Even though the cabin would qualify as a temporary structure under all other criteria, she tells me, it cannot be erected within the curtilage of a listed building without obtaining planning permission. The curtilage is defined as the area within the demesne walls or, more usually, the 'amenity grounds' that would naturally pertain to the house. This would rule out the drive, but also, she thought, the Shrubbery field, where the architects think it might best be located.

I protest that one of the purposes of erecting the log-house for the Kirwans is to allow us more time and freedom to restore and extend the lodge, as the conservation officer herself suggested. She replies that I will have to make this argument as part of my planning application. Even though Susie has lived and worked at Tibradden all her life, the rules on one-off housing in rural areas mean I have to establish her personal case to be housed in this locality. This should be an easy matter so long as the lodge is uninhabitable; but were I to submit a simultaneous planning application for the lodge, the chance of getting permission for the log-house would diminish. Having considered everything, we decide to seek permission for the log-house alone in the first instance.

It's late September and Colin and I are bringing the lambs in from the Nineteen Acres. It is time to separate them into groups of males and females. The females we'll keep up in the Green Gardens to become next year's hoggets. Colin will bring the fatter ram lambs down in Pádraig's trailer to sell at Doyle's mart next Tuesday. They look well to my novice eye, plump around the tail and heavy at the shoulders; you can tell there's Texel in them. One of our farming neighbours confided to me recently that it was a long time since he'd seen lambs this good go out from Guinness's.

'You know we don't have to sell any land at all if we don't want to,' Colin says now, for we've been discussing how we might divide up this field to sell to McNamara. We are standing in front of a lone lichened hawthorn, covered with dripping wet clusters of deepest claret berries. Its leaves are already yellowing, as if donning camouflage to become litter among the conkers in the yellowing stalks of the late-summer grass. To our right, another four hawthorns line up along the ditch clogged with nettles. They, too, would have been planted as whips along the boundary between the townlands of Tibradden and Kilmashogue. Two hundred, two hundred and fifty – how many years have they stood at the edge, exercising their small local claim to hook the world within view?

McNamara's are offering us so much money that if we sell the far side of this field, about twenty acres, we could renovate and extend the lodge, handsomely renovate the main house and Cloragh farmyard, restore the gardens and still have enough money left over to be financially secure for the rest of our lives. We would be rich. I could give up work and spend time with Kim, buy a pony, install a swimming pool and read interiors magazines. Colin could buy a tractor, or we could employ a steward to farm the land for us and amble through it idly instead of herding sheep.

'Look!' Colin grabs my arm, and points out a buzzard rising heavily from among the trees at the redoubt, about a hundred yards distant. We watch it ascend over Pedlows' fields and climb in an arc, the five feathers spread like fingers at the tips of its wings as it soars back over us. A posse of jackdaws clatters up from the woods along the stream and pursues it noisily, making the buzzard drop suddenly and then ascend again in an attempt to shake them off as it tracks back down the valley towards its nest.

15.

Through the autumn, our negotiations with McNamara's have gathered pace. As the emails fly back and forth between their team and mine, I feel strangely disconnected from it all, as though I'm stuck playing for matchsticks in my father's living room while the game has progressed to the tournament tables next door.

On 24 October, Colin and I are called to a meeting at the estate agent's offices. The conference room looks out over the reedy waters of the Grand Canal. The suits glide in and introduce themselves in the hushed tones of corporate etiquette: their lawyers and mine, their accountants and mine, their personal assistants. We exchange warm handshakes before taking our places around the table. McNamara's have sent Mr Noble and another emissary, a Mr Hynes; Bernard McNamara himself is busy, they say. Their manner is straightforward and personable. We are here to agree the final figures that will go into McNamara's letter of offer for the twenty acres they are hoping to buy.

The advisers mostly conduct the discussion among themselves, leaving Colin and me and the two developers on the other side of the table to serve as oddly ceremonial figures. I haven't slept much these past few months: Kim is still waking, and my worries about Susie and Joseph and these negotiations churn around in the early hours seeking resolution. I find it difficult to concentrate. A bronze statue of a colossal barge horse stands bang outside the window opposite and I find my gaze returning to the kitsch figure of a ragged boy standing barefoot at its head. As the meeting wears on, I try to work out whether the boy is deliberately undersized by comparison to the heavy horse he's leading, or whether the odd scale is an accidental error on the part of its maker. It's as if the analytical part of my brain has seized on this problem as a displacement activity for something else, like a crossword puzzle or Sudoku, or one of those Chinese puzzle boxes that require a special series of moves to open it.

I am determined to appear as calm and smiling as any of the other players at the table; but as the advisers move closer to agreeing the terms of a contract, it feels like a noose tightening. Finally I get to ask the question that's been playing on my mind for more than a year now: 'What guarantee do I have that the land I sell will be used for a golf course, and not re-zoned for housing in the next County Development Plan?'

A ripple of demurral spreads about the table. If I facilitate the development of a golf course by selling them this land, the course itself would serve as a bulwark against development pressures in the area, at least in the medium term. I remain unconvinced. After the meeting, I ask Charles's solicitor to find a legal mechanism that would restrict the use of the lands they've already bought to sporting purposes, and to propose this as a condition of my selling them the twenty acres.

A week later, the papers announce that Bernard McNamara is the lead investor in a consortium that has paid €412 million for the site of the former Irish Glass Bottle factory at Ringsend. The consortium wishes to develop a whole new urban quarter on the twenty-four-acre docklands site. At least seven thousand residents will be housed in 2,166 apartments above 826,000 square feet of retail and commercial space tucked in between the candy-striped towers of the Pigeon House and the site of a proposed waste incinerator. The Dublin Docklands Development Authority has also invested heavily in the project. Its involvement means the development can bypass the usual planning process. If this project and our own deal both come to fruition, our view will have McNamara's golfers in the foreground and his Ringsend development in the middle distance, partially obscuring the expanse of Dublin Bay.

McNamara's letter of offer arrives on 7 December. It states that the only restrictive covenant they're prepared to accept is one on constructing any habitable building within seven metres of the River Glin – not much of a concession, and it doesn't rule out cutting down the trees that flank the stream. They add: 'A golf course has manicured fairways and attractive shrubbery and trees and to most individuals would be of benefit, for visual views from their residence, and may even increase the value of adjacent properties.' As a goodwill gesture they are prepared to construct at their own expense the single-storeyed wooden dwelling for which I'm seeking planning permission.

By coincidence, their letter arrives on the very same day we learn of the council's decision to refuse us permission to erect the log-house. The planners deem it unnecessary: with the gate-lodge vacant, and therefore theoretically available for renovation, we have failed to demonstrate a housing need for the Kirwans. They also express their reservations about the intensification of use of our existing 'sub-standard vehicular entrance'. Our architect shakes his head at this: he cannot see how the return of long-time occupants after a brief absence constitutes any 'intensification of use'. He contacts a planning consultant, who advises against our appealing the decision. An Bord Pleanála, he says, currently has a backlog of nine months on planning appeals, and rarely overturns decisions about rural housing in any case. I would be better off abandoning plans for the log-house and putting in an application to redesign and extend the lodge. Whatever my reservations about selling land, if I am to honour my promise to Susie, I now need the McNamara deal to finance it.

In March 2007, we begin to plant a thirty-five-acre deciduous forest in the set-aside fields across the lane. The weather – dry and bright, with overnight ground frosts – is not ideal: the saplings laid out in sacks along the track in the Ladies' Meadows risk drying out before they can be dug in. Oak, beech, ash, sycamore and Wildstar cherry will be interspersed with Scots pine, larch and Douglas fir. These three coniferous species will act as nursery trees to ensure their slower broadleaf cousins grow up straight and strong. 'This is the last time you'll see a private forest on this scale planted within sight of the city,' our forestry consultant, Seán Lenihan, tells the department inspector, when he comes out to check on our progress.

When they start digging, the contractors discover an impermeable hardpan about ten inches below the ground. This hardpan is the legacy of decades of tilling: the plough and the harrow carving and folding the top layer of soil while compacting the acidic clay beneath. It won't be possible to dig trenches in which to plant the trees, so Seán decides to adopt an alternative method whereby holes are dug at close intervals through the fields and the saplings planted by hand in the mounds of earth thrown up on the side. Apparently, the trees will establish their roots more quickly in the looser soil. The disadvantages of this approach become apparent when, out on a walk, I find myself stumbling through a minefield of shallow craters. Seán assures me that, as the root systems grow, the ground will even out.

This plantation is one of two we proposed to the Forestry Service back in the late autumn of 2005. Teagasc had advised me, that difficult summer after Charles died, to consider assigning my unproductive pastures to deciduous forestry, as a way of supplementing our small Single Farm Payment. A government grant would cover the costs of trees, planting and deer fencing, and if the plantations passed inspection and were properly maintained, I would qualify for a tax-free premium for the first twenty years. Further revenue would come from thinnings, but my children's children would see the bulk of the profit at harvest-time.

A year later, Seán Lenihan came up from Wexford to advise me on the project. By that stage, it was clear to me that Joe Kirwan, who had suffered his accident not long before, would not be in a position to go on grazing the Green Gardens for ever. The top two thirds of the field were covered with bracken, and gorse bushes had started to take over the lower pasture, the one Joe had pointed out was missing from my maps. It seemed to me that it would require a lot of work and machinery to put these fields right, and that forestry might be a better option here.

Seán parked his Jeep at the Green Gardens and together we walked up along the road past the entrance to the Coillte forest. We stopped to admire the copse of tall Scots pines standing halfway down the steep slope. My gaze drifted across to the city spread before us. I could see the Hill of Tara and, on the far horizon, the Mournes. 'This is the perfect site to establish a native woodland,' Seán said, scanning the steep incline towards the stream and back up again to the Coillte woods behind us.

Once the department approved our plans, I'd be under no obligation to plant immediately. I could let Joe continue to graze the fields for as long as he wished and keep the forestry plan on the back burner. Before he had started working as

Tibradden's herdsman, Joe had worked up here for the Forestry Service. He had been part of a team of men who had cleared the site with heavy horses, sprayed for weeds, and dug in the Sitka spruce, tree by tree. This history made me hope that Joe might forgive me for eventually planting the fields he grazed.

Back at the house, Seán explained that if I applied to participate in the Native Woodland Scheme, an ecologist would have to complete a survey of the Green Gardens' existing species and draw up a management plan to protect and extend the existing ecosystems. The trees we planted would all have to be native species, grown from indigenous seeds. The copse of mature Scots pine was evidence of earlier afforestation on the site, and suggested this was the main species we should plant. If we were lucky, Seán said, the plantation could attract pine martens, and the endangered crossbills that feed on pine cones. Larch would be the other main species, while rowan, holly and elder, all smaller fruiting species, would provide a rich food supply to over-wintering woodland birds. A fifth of the site, probably the upper section along the lane, would remain unplanted to allow shrub species such as hawthorn and guelder rose to colonize the margins. A dense under-storey of herbs would carpet the glades; hazels, alder and willows along the stream would ripen for coppicing. When the time came to extract timber, individual trees would be harvested by tractor or, given the steep gradient, by cables harnessed to heavy horses.

I should have known by this stage that no decisions about farming Tibradden would ever be easy to implement. The view of the city out across the Green Gardens from Tibradden Lane turned out to be listed for protection in the County Development Plan. Accordingly, the Forestry Service referred our application to the local authority for their consent. Early in the New Year, just as the tragedy of Joe's death unfolded, the planners at Dun Laoghaire/Rathdown decided we would have to obtain planning permission before going ahead with the scheme. As far as Seán Lenihan knew, our plan to plant a native woodland in the Green Gardens was the first of twelve thousand forestry applications to be singled out by a local authority to go through the full planning process. He advised me to talk to the planners.

Over the phone, I explained that we had already taken the view into consideration in our plans for the site. We would be happy to show how, by planting along the gradient, we could preserve the panorama from the top of the lane. The planner, unconvinced, suggested I engage a firm of consultants to prepare a full environmental-impact statement on how the view might be affected when the trees reached maturity. 'That will be fifty years hence for larch, eighty for Scots pine,' I said, commending her department's ability to think so far ahead. I wondered aloud how close the city would have come by then, and with what effect. We couldn't afford the cost of consultants, on top of the routine expenses of the planning process, so we had to abandon these plans for the Green Gardens and confine our forestry planting to the set-aside fields. The absurdity of this situation resonates more loudly now that I'm fighting for a covenant to protect trees from a developer whose ambitions seem to meet little opposition.

In early April, McNamara's team propose significant changes to the deal. Instead of buying the twenty acres outright, they now wish to buy just four acres initially and take out an option on the remainder for eighteen months. The four acres are contiguous with the land-bank they already own. If, at the end of the eighteen-month period, they decide not to buy the other sixteen acres, then I keep the option deposit. In addition, as a goodwill gesture, they would like to offer me €100,000 towards the refurbishment of the lodge, for which we now, at last, have the architect's plans.

The estate agent attributes the developers' change of tack primarily to jitters in the local golf club about transferring to Tibradden: members are worried about the inclines on some of the fairways. But McNamara's have promised to address these concerns in a new design, and the agent shares their conviction that a deal can yet be done. When I ask whether he considers the revised offer evidence that the property market is about to crash, as some economists are now predicting, he assures me that any stagnation in the market is only temporary. Nonetheless, he thinks it would be wise to accept the option arrangement. This would at least guarantee me some return for the months of negotiation in the event of a sale on the larger part falling through.

During May, the solicitors work on drafting a contract of sale on the four acres and an option agreement on the sixteen. In the exchange, there is much toing and froing over my request for a covenant to protect the trees along the River Glin; eventually McNamara's agree to a clause committing them to preserve 'the deciduous and continuous character of the existing riparian woodland'. Once the land is surveyed and the area mapped and agreed, we can arrange a meeting to shake on the deal and sign.

All seems in order. Except that one evening, around this time, I run into a local councillor at a book launch. She tells me that back in January she attended a debate on the provision of affordable housing co-hosted by three of her Green Party colleagues, John Gormley, Eamon Ryan and Ciarán Cuffe. Among those on the panel was Bernard McNamara. Her ears pricked up when he announced that, if the Affordable Housing Partnership were serious about reducing the waiting list for social and affordable homes in the Dun Laoghaire/Rathdown area, he had a site of more than a hundred acres in Kilmashogue that he would make available. In return for re-zoning, he promised to build 700 units for the local authority with an additional 300 units for sale on the open market. She tells me the *Irish Independent* published an article about McNamara's proposal shortly afterwards, but I haven't heard about it until now.

I leave the book launch feeling shocked and betrayed. I've always doubted that a golf course was the height of McNamara's ambitions for our land, but when I put this to his people there was never any mention of the sort of development he talked about at the Green Party meeting. I ask the estate agent what he knew of all this, and he replies: 'I'm sure Bernard was just flying a kite.' Yet when I do my own digging, I discover that McNamara has good cause to think a thousand-unit housing development on our hillside might be viable. By applying directly to the Affordable Housing Partnership, developers can circumvent the usual planning process to get their land re-zoned for residential schemes that meet the Partnership's criteria for affordability and the provision of infrastructure and services. When a scheme is approved, the board makes a strong recommendation to the local authority to re-zone the land for housing. Five county managers sit on the Partnership's board, including the county manager of Dun Laoghaire/Rathdown. Given the strength of this representation, it seems unlikely that councillors would reject a recommendation from the Partnership, particularly in our own county where waiting lists for affordable housing have trebled over the past few years.

Recently, at a local event, I met the man responsible for building Ballycullen, a suburban estate not far from here. He seemed a genuinely nice and decent man. 'It's fashionable now for people to give out about builders,' he told me, 'but look at all the lovely green space we left in that development for children to play on.' And since our conversation, whenever I drive down the Gunny Hill behind Ballycullen, I dutifully peer through the tall mounted railings on my right and recall my own childhood playing out on greens just like these. On the other side of the road are hawthorn hedgerows strewn with litter, and through the gaps I glimpse cattle grazing on thick lush pastures. It seems frankly unethical to lament, on aesthetic grounds alone, the transformation of this winding rural hill-road into an ugly scar where farmland and suburb are sutured together. I must accept that this is how all cities stutter out at their margins. This is the territory where farming lives suddenly seem anachronistic and expendable. I have struggled to try to provide better living conditions for Susie and Joseph, so why do I find it so difficult to accept another man's ambition to provide the same on a much more effective and sustainable scale?

In mid-June, the rain doesn't stop. In anticipation of a deal with McNamara's we have secured a mortgage to re-roof the house, rebuild the chimneys, and repair the thirty-one windows. After removing the slates and securing a PVC membrane in their place, the roofers disappear for three weeks. Our architect fears they've gone to another job, and promises to do his best to get them back on site. A black patch begins to appear on the ceiling of Mel's room as the rain pours down. A Pole and a sleep-deprived Lithuanian appear one afternoon and spend an hour up on the scaffolding, hammering down loose corners of the membrane. It is not enough. On 22 June we get an entire month's rainfall in a single day. Water seeps into Kim's room and our bedroom, and then, after lunch, I notice it is pouring in above the spare bedroom window. I go to fetch buckets and towels when the doorbell rings. It is Gerry Farrell come to set a date for his joiners to start work on the windows. 'What's up, chicken?' he asks. He follows me up the stairs, opens the window and matter-of-factly climbs out onto the scaffolding, and shouts, 'You've a reservoir dammed up here.' He steps aside to release a cascade safely down through the scaffolding below.

That night Colin and I listen to the roar of the stream from our bedroom. Next morning, our water tank is empty. When Colin goes up to investigate, he discovers the pipe has been washed away, and the stream is now a river that would take him, too, if he stepped down to look further. He walks back down Larch Hill's avenue and tracks the river through the Nineteen Acres. When he reaches the place where the old boating pond used to be, he discovers a scene of ecological carnage. The river has carved a canyon through the silt at the place where Charles and my father once fished. Where it met resistance, the water surged straight into the field, flinging a tangle of trees and branches and rocks across its entirely new shores. The canyon is about ten feet wide and twenty deep. We have lost a great area of pasture.

Further downstream, things are worse. Our parish makes the front page of the *Irish Times* as the epicentre of a localized extreme weather event. The fire brigade evacuated residents along Whitechurch Road overnight and Taylor's Lane is closed. Much of Rathfarnham is still a foot under water.

A few days later, Colin encounters an insurance assessor out walking in the Nineteen Acres. He reports that tonnes of silt have wrecked the greens of a local golf course, about a mile downstream, and he's on a mission to find its source. 'I can help you there,' Colin says, and leads him over to the canyon. The assessor finds it hard to credit that the stream below ever had the power to move so much earth. As they stand together, marvelling at the force of nature, the irony occurs to Colin that while the members of this same golf club deliberate about relocating here, the field itself has given up waiting for their decision and gone to them.

Susie, too, seems to have given up waiting. In April I asked her if she would like to see the new plans for the lodge. She thought about it for a moment before replying quietly that she didn't think she would. I took her reply to mean she had lost faith in my commitment to see her return home. Her habitual enquiries after my parents and my maternal grandmother had grown frostier. On the way down to the nursing home, I would rack my brain for local news to tell her, but this ran out quickly, and after I received perfunctory answers to my questions about her and Joseph's welfare there was little for it but to sit beside each other on the floral sofa and talk about the weather.

When I could, I brought Kim. Now that he was walking and making animal noises, he could sometimes raise the ghost of a smile from Susie, but it was Joseph who really loved seeing him. He had alarmed me, the first time I'd brought the baby in, by lurching over and thrusting his face right into the car-seat and then raising his hand. I started forward but instead of the incidental act of violence I feared – for I'd seen Joseph gleefully hurl plates and glasses across the room – he ran his fingers over my son's soft blond hair, and then lowered his forehead, very, very gently, to rest on Kim's. I realized then that for him to show such affection, so delicately, so carefully, was evidence, too, of his own parents' love.

I had faltered when explaining why the council had refused us permission to erect the log-house, for I couldn't find a way to fit their bureaucratic logic to any frame of decency Susie could understand. She had noticed me falter, and tucked this observation away to herself, to mull over in her solitary hours. She suspected, it seemed to me, that I'd played her for a fool, plotting with the HSE to get her evicted and keep her in a nursing home until she died and Joseph could be put in care, which was, she said to me once, all that anyone seemed to want.

Now, at the height of summer, the HSE has reconvened the Kirwans' case conference. A recent biopsy has revealed that Susie's cancer has returned. There are inoperable lesions on her lungs and liver, and she has been readmitted to hospital to receive palliative treatment. The case team are focused on finding a residential place for Joseph and settling on a plan for his long-term care. The Kirwans' friend John has visited a home in Stamullen, County Meath, which specifically caters for adults with Joseph's range of intellectual disability. He thinks it would be ideal. Needless to say, there is no longer any question of their returning to the lodge. When I ask the team whether I should offer to take Susie back home some afternoon, they advise against it. The visit would be too distressing. It would be kinder to let her remember Tibradden the way it was.

When I go in to visit her in hospital, she greets me warmly. Her sole concern is Joseph and who's minding him and how she will see him before she dies. I tell her that the owners of the nursing home are already preparing a separate room for her to convalesce in, where Joseph can visit every day for as long as she wants. Pádraig has given me a punnet of strawberries for her from his pick-your-own fruit farm, and we sit there together, eating strawberries that were grown in the field adjacent to Joe's at Cruagh. When I get up to leave, she asks me when I think I'll be able to visit her again. 'Soon, Susie,' I promise, 'very soon.'

Although the map outlining the area to be sold was agreed and finalized in mid-July, by September we still haven't signed a deal. Each draft contract returns with changes we have not agreed. Charles's solicitor is no longer sure whether the successive revisions are evidence that McNamara's board are overruling their own negotiating team, or whether the other side is playing for time because the contracts with the golf club have yet to be signed. The latest revision is the introduction of a gagging clause: in signing it, I would give up my right to lodge an objection to any planning application McNamara's might make on the lands they own. The estate agent tells me that such clauses have become standard practice. The precise wording of the clause becomes the subject of more argument and counter-argument between solicitors through late summer and into autumn.

Through all this, without fuss, my husband has been farming. In mid-August he brought a batch of six lambs down to O'Gorman's abattoir in Castledermot. A fortnight later he collected them bagged and ready for delivery to our first private customers for Tibradden lamb. Most are friends and colleagues who view this fresh challenge to Colin's vegetarianism with sympathetic amusement. Somehow, while I've been farming paper and electronic landscapes in the form of maps and emails, he's been quietly attending to the real thing.

And I know there's no way back when Colin opens his laptop one evening to show me the website of the British Coloured Sheep Breeders Association. Its homepage has a picture of a black ewe with a white blaze down her face, four white socks and a white-tipped tail. 'I've found us a Mod sheep,' he says delightedly. The markings of the Zwartbles breed apparently echo the striped bowling shoes worn by Paul Weller on a certain episode of *The Old Grey Whistle Test* many years ago. 'They'll look good at the mart in Blessington,' I say, but Colin is undeterred by my wifely sarcasm. He sets off in the Land Rover a few days later for Roscommon to purchase the Zwartbles ram lamb he saw advertised serendipitously in the *Farmers Journal*. Oscar, for so Mel has named him despite our reservations about what a Wildean ram might do for our ewes, has taken up residence in the courtyard. He joins our new sheepdog: a small blue merle pup with one brown eye, one blue, called Bowie.

By the end of September, my thoughts are elsewhere. My mother is marrying her partner of fifteen years and the wedding is to be in France. She has asked me to make a speech at their reception. I am told the wedding is for adults only, so I will be flying out on my own on Friday morning to return home Sunday evening. It has been a busy week and I'm hoping to write the speech on the plane.

On Thursday afternoon I am down in the kitchen playing with Kim when Pádraig calls. 'I'm just ringing to find out the arrangements,' he begins.

'What for?' I ask.

There's a long pause. 'Have you not heard?' Another neighbour has just called to tell him Susie passed away this morning.

My son's insistent voice sings out his new word, 'Yo-ghurt.' I fetch it from the fridge, open the drawer, fetch the spoon, sit him in his chair, open the lid, pass it to him. I find I can do all this automatically. Pádraig tells me Susie was readmitted to hospital on Monday. My mind slides from the news of her death to Joseph. Have they told him yet? I wonder, and then realize it's the wrong question to ask. He'll understand her absence, eventually.

I ring John to find out more. As much as such a thing can be said to exist, he thinks Susie died a good death. Her old neighbour Eddie was in with her the night before, and she told him all about her father's people in Avoca. The funeral will be held after ten o'clock mass on Saturday in Ballyroan church; she will be buried alongside Joe in the small cemetery at Cruagh. I explain why it won't be possible for me to attend.

On the early flight to Toulouse, I find it almost impossible to compose the proper sentiments for my mother's nuptials. I keep wondering about Joseph, what form his loss will take. For the moment, John told me, he'll stay on in the Dun Laoghaire nursing home and continue attending day-care at St Michael's House. Soon, though, it will be time for him to move again. How much of his story will go with him on the journey to Stamullen? Without people or place, I imagine the bale of twine unspooling as he travels, that blue thread his last connection to Tibradden.

16.

Over a year has passed since last we sat in this conference room, overlooking the canal. No contract of sale or option agreement has yet been signed. Twice we arranged to meet and sign contracts at their solicitors' offices. Twice these meetings were cancelled on the day due to some last-minute confusion over figures. The estate agent's emails became increasingly urgent: 'Get it signed, the market is wretched and cash is short!' Then everything went ominously quiet for about a fortnight until we were called in to this meeting today. The golf-course plan has gone belly-up, the estate agent explained, but McNamara's have new plans for the land, which they'd like to present to us.

Mr Hynes and a colleague of his we've never met before, Mr Gallagher, greet us warmly. There are no lawyers present. We take our seats and the two McNamara's men position themselves by the flip-chart.

Mr Hynes explains that, the golf-club deal having collapsed, they now hope to make an application through the Affordable Housing Partnership to have the St Thomas land re-zoned for housing. They propose building about a thousand residential units, of which about 70 per cent will be 'affordable homes' for gardaí, nurses, teachers and young executives. He takes great pains to distinguish between the lists for 'social housing' and 'affordable housing'. I ask whether

I've misunderstood the scheme's mandatory condition that 10 per cent of the development must be allocated to social housing. He admits this is true, but the social-housing provision will be grouped away from our property towards Kilmashogue Lane. Like a ghetto? I suggest. No, more a recognition of the different needs of society. Sports fields and leisure facilities will be located at that end of the site; a twenty-one-acre park will wrap around the end of the development nearest us. The family homes they propose building for the private market will open out onto this amenity and so will be located at our end. At the centre of the development will be a village green with community services and shops. All in all, they expect to accommodate a population of 2,500 to 3,000 in what they describe as a low-density village. More detailed plans will be drawn up by Tengbom, the Swedish firm of architects who have established an international reputation for environmental sensitivity through their design of a new suburb outside Stockholm, named Hammarby.

We have been playing this game for so long, it comes as a relief finally to see their hand. If it has to be housing, I'd prefer a development of affordable homes designed and built on a sustainable model to a posh gated estate. And, as I read it, this scheme offers safeguards about community provision, which might prevent a developer from leaving a population marooned on the mountainside without proper transport and infrastructure.

Although this area is rural in appearance, I am conscious that it is viewed as a sort of picturesque variant on suburbia by a growing proportion of the people who live here. When we planted the top set-aside field with cherry, oak and beech, one neighbour came to object that she had moved to the countryside to look at animals, not trees. If she wanted trees, she said, she could go to Marlay Park. Another wanted me to mow down the yarrow and cow parsley growing along our verges and replace these 'weeds' with grass seed to keep the lane looking trim.

Now I wonder whether I was right to go ahead and afforest the set-aside fields, if a new suburb is to be slapped up against our land on this side of the lane, for it means we've fewer pastures for grazing livestock away from harm. I fear dog-attacks on our sheep, and trespassers casually climbing through the fences and hedges that we'll have to patch up after them. I fear rubbish being slung over garden walls into our fields for the animals to choke on. Beyond these practical worries lurk other sorrows such as the loss of our dark nights to the glow of apartment blocks and street lighting, or the loss of habitat for wildlife – such as the seven hares I spotted with Kim one day in the Nineteen Acres. And then there is the quiet rush that stretches out around you in the fields, a rush full of sounds, elemental, animal, human, without the distorting top notes of house and car alarms. And beyond all of this is a sense of grief for the lost texture of stories, and names, that clothe these fields like a blanket pulled up tight around a child on a cold night, and which I'd been hoping to tuck around Kim.

Now, Mr Hynes and Mr Gallagher explain, they would like me to consider selling them our silage field, the Lower Lawn – preferably as a direct swap for the section of the Nineteen Acres that's been under discussion for the past twelve months. The estate agent suggests we might like to throw in the walled Calfpark, too, a field no one has mentioned till now. It would prove the ideal location for a school to serve the new development. I sense Colin is about to lose patience with the endless shifting of goalposts, and under the table I press his leg hard. They are still offering to buy the four-acre bit of the Nineteen Acres, minus the option on the rest, and I don't think we can afford to lose this deal. I worry that if we prove in any way difficult, they may seek to make the sale of the four acres conditional on selling them these other fields. So I tell them we'll consider it, but add that at this stage, if negotiations are to continue, we need a gesture of good faith. The contract for the four acres must be signed within the next two weeks.

Four days later, a neighbour phones. 'I've a copy of the *Southside People* here. Let me read you what it says on the front page.' He clears his throat before reading me the headline: 'Politicians oppose attempts to re-zone Dublin Mountain lands.' The report includes interviews with two opponents of the scheme: Ciarán Fallon, a Green Party councillor, who says that Dun Laoghaire/Rathdown already has sufficient land zoned to meet its affordable housing targets; and Olivia Mitchell, a Fine Gael TD, who describes the plan as 'a step too far'. 'It says here,' he continues, 'that the developers are seeking "a fast-track approach such as a material contravention or a variation of the development plan to save two or two and half years in the process of providing over six hundred units of affordable housing". What does that mean?' He breaks off. 'Can I ask you did you know about this?'

'Yes,' I tell him, 'since Monday last.'

A few days later I have a similar conversation with another neighbour when the *Sunday Business Post* follows up the story in a separate article.

In the evenings, when the house is quiet, Colin and I sit up and take stock of our finances. We've fixed the roof and the windows, rebuilt the chimney stacks and replaced the gutters, shot-blasted the exterior to remove the dirt and rust stains, and repainted the house a shade of pink that we thought was marshmallow until the scaffolding came down and revealed it to be more like the colour of Germolene. Inside, we've rewired and replumbed, removed the dry rot from the basement and asbestos lagging from the pipes, taken down the landing ceiling that had absorbed a decade of leaks and put it up again. Structurally, the house is now sound, apart from our chimneys, which need to be relined at a cost of €8,000 apiece before we dare to light fires. This is more than we can afford to do at the moment. The hall, dining room and drawing room are still decorated in the best wartime utility colours available to my grandmother when the rooms were last done in 1940. Her curtains still hang in the ground-floor windows, stained and ragged from decades of sun, damp and dust.

In addition to this, there's the lodge. When, in the summer, we found out that Susie and Joseph would not be coming home, the project moved down our list of priorities. But then in October, when McNamara's seemed ready to sign, I told the architects to go ahead and pull together a planning application for their design to extend the lodge into a fully accessible, three-bedroom house. One day, Colin and I may want to live in a more manageable home and pass the baton of the main house to our children. Until that time arrives, we could let it out to tenants, who might inhabit the place with their happier stories. But none of this will come to pass without money. By 4 December when the estate agent calls, we've reconciled ourselves to selling the Lower Lawn.

But yet again the goalposts have shifted. Mr Hynes has told him that the bank is no longer prepared to advance McNamara's the price they offered us. As a result, they are no longer interested in buying any portion of the Nineteen Acres, but want instead to buy the Lower Lawn for exactly half the price per acre we'd agreed before.

Apart from the money and my own frustration at all the wasted time and speculation, there is another reason to reconsider selling. If I let them have this corner field, they will own pretty much the entire length of Tibradden Road down to Kilmashogue roundabout. When I drive this road, I feel like I am caressing the bends as they trace every twist and turn of our estate wall. The map of 1811, drawn for Sarah Davis, shows this wall already in place, planted along its length with oaks, field maples, elms, beeches and the occasional fir as a nursery tree. At the bend identified as the site-access point on the map that accompanied the *Sunday Business Post* article, a lone fir tree stands, looking as if it were planted precisely to make the road divert around it. It's not a particularly elegant specimen: its upper branches have been knocked about by the wind so it tilts a little towards the hill. I don't expect it will survive for long. Just up from it is a spot where the levels in the St Thomas fields are about three feet higher than the road. Sometimes cows appear to levitate over the wall, their long tongues searching out the clover that grows in the cracks of the limestone mortar now exposed to the weather by the loss of its capping stones. I walked this road with Charles that first winter when I'd just started school at St Columba's. We put our bags in a red plastic toboggan and my uncle pulled it behind him as he tried to keep his balance on the ice in his ordinary shoes. I know that if I sell them this field, there will be nothing to prevent them from removing this wall and straightening this road to meet the requisite sightlines for the entrance to their new development. Robert Frost once said there was something in nature 'that doesn't love a wall', and 'spills the upper boulders in the sun'. Perhaps. But I feel like his neighbour, 'the old-stone savage', who goes out to mend it with him, armed with sayings from his father. Fearing the destruction of the wall and all it represents, I tell the agent to let McNamara's know, as politely as he sees fit, that they can go to hell with their deals and negotiations. I'll find another way of raising the money we require.

Hearing my husband's voice outside, I get up from my desk and go to stand by the window. In the field, Colin stands with a small flock of our hoggets and the pup, Bowie. He is wearing a flat cap and a waxed jacket. 'Come by, come by, come by,' he shouts, as the dog streaks off after a breaking sheep and turns it back towards the flock. It's drizzling, and the Lawn is ragged with leaves. The lime tree describes its beautiful bell curve, its branches a network of capillaries that leach into the distant suburbs at their ends.

'Mummy?' says Kim, coming into the room, wearing the Spiderman suit he got a few days ago for his second birthday. 'I want see man flying.' Last week I took him to Fossett's circus at Kilmainham and his mouth fell open gazing at the acrobats twirling round the tent, suspended on the lengths of fabric they had twisted round their arms. I lift him up to watch his daddy in the field below. 'Bo,' he says, pointing at the dog.

'That's right, Bowie.' He practises the word, pouting his lips in a big round 'O'. Out on the landing, above our laundry basket, hangs a portrait of Charles painted when he was four or five years old. He is wearing a blue frilly shirt and matching knickerbockers, and his heavy blond fringe falls across his brow. His mouth is set in the same stern pout he pulled all his life to express surprise. Kim looks just like him now.

It is time for me to fetch his coat and mine, and to drive down to Ballinteer to collect Mel from school. I carry him down to the kitchen, and find my woollen coat behind the door. It smells strongly of sheep and is splashed with mud. I put it on anyway and bring Kim out through the scullery, which is littered with feeding tubes, buckets, pet food and a spilt tub of powdered colostrum. Discarded boots and a pair of water-proof trousers lie on the floor. I inhale, and wrinkle my nose at the heavy agricultural smell, warm and rancid, clammy and close.

17.

From the outside, the nursing home where Joseph now lives looks like an ordinary apartment complex. A nurse gets up from the reception desk to let me in and invites me to take a seat and wait for her colleague.

When Patricia and I cleared out the lodge, we discovered a Wills Gold Flake tobacco tin full of cards and recipes and letters, and two black-and-white photographs. The first shows Susie standing at the top of the drive flanked by two men. She might be in her forties, and looks well: her hair, parted firmly on the left, descends just below her ears in a tidy wave. She is wearing an ill-fitting striped suit with a flared skirt and long jacket, which has popped a button at the bust. A black Labrador is sitting at her feet, panting. Her long arms hang slackly down, relaxed, and her mouth is set in an intelligent smile for the camera. From the way she is positioned, just slightly ahead of the two men, you'd know she was in charge.

The second photograph looks to have been taken on the day of Joe and Susie's wedding. The bride is wearing a stout tweed suit with a black fur stole crossed neatly round her neck, all topped off with a silk turban hat of a kind my grandmother used to favour for formal occasions. The three-quarter-length sleeves show off her black leather gloves. A polished black handbag dangles from the crook of her left elbow, so that her left hand can guard her front where the jacket slightly tautens.

She stands straight and proud, her right hand looped through her bridegroom's arm. He is some four inches shorter and his posture is a bit crooked, but he is dressed equally smartly in a dark three-piece suit and narrow tie. They are standing, flanked by their two witnesses, in a field with daisies scattered through the long grass. There are no houses in sight, just a hill rising behind the hedgerow flush with ripe elderflowers. Some young conifers are visible on the right, and it's these trees – planted by Joe when he worked in the forestry – that help me identify this setting as the Green Gardens. None of the members of the wedding party are smiling broadly, nor do they seem unhappy. There is an air of resolution about the event.

A staff nurse called Trudy comes out to greet me. Before we go in to see him, I ask her what she knows of Joseph's background. 'Very little,' she says. They know that he lived with his mother in a nursing home in Dun Laoghaire, but before that they've had to piece together clues. 'One of the girls here wondered whether he lived on a farm. He can imitate all the animals so perfectly. When he barks, you'd think there was a dog behind you, and sometimes he calls out for Lassie.'

Each of the residents has a folder for his or her personal effects, she says. If I like, she can show me Joseph's. I follow her down the bright, cheery corridor to his bedroom, sit down on the chair by his bed and leaf through the pages of his folder. There are good-luck cards from the residents and staff of the Dun Laoghaire nursing home, pictures of Joseph with other residents at his previous home in Stamullen, and then the picture I took of Susie the week before she left the lodge, looking haggard, sitting in the big armchair in the drawing room, with Kim in his christening robes spread out across her lap. It is the only photograph of either parent in his folder.

Trudy leads me into a large recreational area, with a television room off to one side, couches along the walls, and a ballpool at one end where one of the residents is rolling around with a big grin on her face, while another watches her over the top of a drum kit he's playing with the aid of a nurse. Joseph is sitting on the floor, twiddling a long loop of blue baler twine. I sit down beside him, and he squints at me closely, then encircles my head in his arm and brings my forehead down very gently to meet his: his greeting. The punnet of strawberries I've brought him is confiscated by a passing nurse who returns them chopped in a bowl, explaining, 'He has a weak swallow.' He pops them into his mouth, one after another, in quick succession.

When he has finished, I take out the two photographs and pass them over carefully. He takes the first and brings it up close until it touches his nose. 'There's your mother, Joseph. That picture was taken before you were born.' I pass him the second. 'There's your dad too, with your mum the day they were married.' He peers hard at them. I'd hoped he might show some sign of recognition, some sign of a private memory, but after a moment he discards them casually on the floor and feels around for the baler twine. 'Would you get him another bit of twine, Joe?' he sings out suddenly, his voice not his own, but his mother's, pitch perfect and exact.

Epilogue

April 2012

Nothing has yet happened to the lands below us. Cattle and sheep still graze in the fields. The trees along the stream still wave their spring colours in the wind.

In June 2008, McNamara's submitted their forty-page masterplan for what they called Kilmashogue Village to Dun Laoghaire/Rathdown council. Their brochure showed rows of terraces with three- and four-bed duplexes, and residential blocks with internal courtyards, all serviced by a main street running east to west across the site. Semi-detached houses were to be built at the upper end of the long field below the Lawn, with terraces taking over about halfway down, where the old gate was that I used to climb over as a schoolgirl on those lost walks home. The plan contained a number of environmentally friendly features: many of the blocks were to have 'living roofs', planted with sedum, and solar panels to provide hot water. There was to be a central sewage-treatment facility that would separate out sludge material to convert into biogas, with the residue processed as fertilizer. Refuse chutes were to be 'linked by underground pipes to a central collection station by air vacuum', where the compostable waste would be sorted out and used for biogas while the combustible rubbish would be incinerated in the development's own power plant to supply heat and electricity.

But by the summer of 2008, the tide had turned decisively

against the property developers. Prices were falling dramatically and the banks were no longer lending. And the era of re-zoning agricultural land for housing was coming to an end. The final draft of the Dun Laoghaire/Rathdown County Development Plan was published in March 2009. In it, the lands at Kilmashogue retained their agricultural zoning. In November 2010, Bernard McNamara's flagship firm, Michael McNamara Construction, went into receivership, shortly followed by Grattan Property and a number of his other development companies. Many of McNamara's loans were taken over by the National Asset Management Agency. To date, the fields below us have not been advertised for sale in its lists of enforced properties. When they are, perhaps the rise in factory prices for beef and lamb might enable some local farmer to buy them for grazing.

Down at the lodge, the builders are busy laying the concrete slab for the extension. It took us two years of negotiation before our bank would approve a mortgage to carry out this work. The Ukrainian who owns the building firm has already been up to enquire about the practicalities of keeping sheep. He has recently bought land in Glencullen where he thinks the grass might be getting out of hand. 'Do they trouble you greatly?' he asks.

The cedars along our drive have had to come down. I remember Joe pointing out those that were balding at the crown. In the intervening years, both rows have died back considerably. Beneath them, dog violets star the grassy turf purple, where once the heavy verdigris branches starved them of rain and light. Three came down of their own accord, and then, at the start of the year, I counted five that were just deadwood standing and knew their ivied trunks would prove a sail to the wind in the next summer storms. Yellow toadstools appeared around one stump in autumn, the fruiting bodies of the dreaded honey fungus, or so I supposed until we started felling. The tree surgeon peeled back the bark on the first trunks to search for white mycelium and, finding none, started to explore the soil for evidence of the bootlace rhizomorphs that spread through the ground. In the absence of any evidence that the honey fungus had taken hold as fiercely as I'd presumed, he began to count the tree's rings. He stopped at 140 and said, 'I think these beauties have just reached the end of their natural lives.' Even so, I didn't have the heart to fell them all, and asked him to leave the best three standing. They might yet last another few years, and serve as a reminder of what once was here. When their time comes, I will replace them with lime trees for coming generations to enjoy the summer sound of honeybees hard at work.

Through February the drive looked like a logging road, with great trunks stacked on either side. In the end, I minded the loss of the cedars less than I expected. It returned the drive to how it must have looked in the 1870s when they were first planted: an airy and open farm track for the carts to roll up.

The tree surgeon chipped all the branches, his machine spitting out pieces into tall heaps among the rhododendrons. Kim, now six, and his brother Ivor, nearly two and curly-headed, love climbing them and tossing the chippings into the air. They come back fragrant with incense as if their play had anointed them the trees' rightful heirs.

It took four lorry-loads to transport all the timber to the saw-mill in Wicklow. There it is being kiln-dried and sawn into lengths, before travelling back on its return journey to Gerry Farrell's yard. He will plane the boards down and turn them into beams and cladding for the new part, and windows and doors throughout, so one day we might retire to a gate-lodge built from the cedars that grew up on site.

Sixty days a year, Tibradden is open to the public. This allows us to claim tax relief on the costs of restoring and running the place. When I welcome visitors into the hall, I watch them take in the shabby splendour of the plasterwork and the marble pillars, the dusty portraits and flaking paint and the crack that runs up to the ceiling above the mirror hung to reflect the light from the arched window on the stairs. The main splendour is behind them, out through the front door, where the land unscrolls towards the city in a succession of fields and parkland, all pretty much unchanged since the house was built. Sooner or later, their gaze will settle and I'll be asked to tell them the story of the crocodile that stands guard by the door.

Acknowledgements

I gratefully acknowledge the financial assistance of An Chomhairle Ealaíon/The Arts Council, the Tyrone Guthrie Centre at Annaghmakerrig and the support of IADT, Dun Laoghaire. The encouragement and expert interventions of my editor, Brendan Barrington, have proved invaluable. I'd like to thank him and all the team at Penguin Ireland.

Professor Michael Cronin and Thea Gillen at Boston College-Ireland most generously lent me an office to get started. Brid Cannon, Jocelyn Clarke, Catríona Clutterbuck, Antonia Edgerton, Siobhán Garrigan, Lavinia Greacen, Aiden Grenelle, Elisabeth and Niall Guinness, Barbara Hughes, Michael Muench, Díóg O'Connell, Justin Quinn, Anne-Marie Ridge and Sarah Searson urged me towards the finishing line through their tactful enquiries, discreet understanding and good example. I would like to acknowledge the enormous part played by Phyllis Byrne, Naomi Mulligan, Giselle Minehane and Sally Comerford, who minded my children so well alongside their own.

I hope this story will testify to the kindness and patience of our friends, relations and neighbours. Conversations with Maisie Williams, Pat Lambert, Rose Flanagan, Richard Ryan and Margaret Judge helped me to understand better the place we call home. Without Pádraig Lambert's friendship and assistance, there would be little of a farm story to tell. I'm indebted to two local histories: Ernie Shepherd's book *Behind the Scenes: The Story of Whitechurch District in South County Dublin* (Whitechurch Publications), and Frank Tracy's *If Those Trees Could Speak: the Story of an Ascendancy Family in Ireland* (South Dublin County Libraries, 2009). Kevin McKenna and Senia Pašeta advised me on how best to use Irish historical sources. I'd like to thank Jim Shannon and James Lyons for their hospitality in Carlow and their assistance in researching a chapter of family history that will appear elsewhere.

My father, Paul Guinness, proved a steady guide on the documentary trail of Tibradden's history. Even more importantly, he stepped aside and allowed me to make this place, his family and their story my own. I owe him a debt of love and gratitude beyond words. Without the company of Mel Graham, Kim and Ivor Guinness, and their father, Colin Graham, life at Tibradden would be thin and unexciting. My greatest thanks, and love, belong to them.